To Jeannie with much l...

Abe

ABE, SON OF ABRAHAM

ABE, SON OF ABRAHAM

Stories, Vignettes, Remembrances, Reflections,
Thoughts & Tributes

By Abe J. Bassett

Library of Congress Control Number: 2014932155

ISBN: 978-0615939391
ISBN: 0615939392

Published by Bayswater-Queensway Books
4085 Danern Drive
Beavercreek, Ohio 45430

Cover design by Elizabeth A. Kelly

1st Printing, February, 2014

Printed in the
United States of America
By CreateSpace

Also by Abe J. Bassett

Memories of Rahija
Library of Congress
CT275.B3794 M45 1992
http://lccn.loc.gov/93205249

Available at and online at
Wright State University Dunbar Library

Through Inter Library Service from
Allen County Public Library
Fort Wayne, Indiana

PREFACE

This collection of vignettes and stories does not purport to be a biography, though many details of my life and family's lives are revealed. The idea of writing life stories first came from Jack and Anne Rutherdale, he my former brother-in-law, and she his second wife. The actual writing of the stories in this book began in an informal class on writing life stories —"One Story At a Time"—led by my friend Robert Wagley of Wright State University.

My first entries were about my early life in Williamson, West Virginia, and more importantly, my relationship with my father. I had previously collected and edited a book of memories of my mother, publishing them as *Memories of Rahija (1992).* Some of my accounts of my mother in that publication are included in this collection. *Memories of Rahija* is available via interlibrary loan or through the Wright State University Dunbar Library CORE collection.

Although the stories in the present collection span the length of my life, the emphasis is on my early years, and my personal growth as a human being. As my career in education spanned thirty-four years, I could not avoid relating highlights of those years.

My Lebanese heritage is revealed not only through the stories of my father and mother, but also through those of my parent's brothers and sisters. My uncles and aunts are a vital part of my history.

The primary intended audience is my immediate family but also future descendants. In addition to stories of my life's events, I have included other items that define me, and the era in which I lived. Those additional items include letters I wrote, tributes delivered at life celebrations of family, my academic resumé, and most importantly, remembrances of my father and mother's siblings and their known history from the town and country of their origin: Kfeir Zeit, Lebanon.

In the future when family genealogists see names on a chart, they will be able to flesh out those names by learning the events and situations that give life to the names. My extended family data is now preserved on the genealogy program, Family Tree Maker. It is my hope that these records will be improved upon and maintained by subsequent generations.

My deepest gratitude is given to my niece Jan Allegra Rutherdale for her encouragements and for doing first edit on many of the stories, and a final comprehensive edit. My wife, Sharon Kinnaird Bassett, gave invaluable editorial advice in addition to unending encouragement and support.

I also acknowledge and thank those who reacted to some of these stories; Robert and Lorraine Wagley, Don Kelsay, Megan Bush, Rachel Magdalene, Nancy Griffith, and Jan Sherman and Patti Russo.

DEDICATION

As these vignettes were arranged into logical groupings, I came to realize how deeply my father shaped my life. The lessons I absorbed in the first two decades of life permeated my being and fashioned my behavior. This awareness led to the title of this book in which I recognize that I am indeed the son of my father. Thus, it is to the memory of my father, Abraham Joseph Bassett, that I dedicate this book.

TABLE OF CONTENTS

I | *GROWING UP WITH PAPA*

WILLIAMSON, THE GREATEST TOWN IN THE WORLD

In the eyes of a young person, Williamson, West Virginia was the greatest town in the world! And it was an important town, too. If the Germans were going to bomb any place in the United States it would be Williamson, West Virginia. When we had practice air raid warnings, we pulled the shades as far down as they would go and we rushed around the house to make sure the lights were off. Then I would sneak outside to make sure no light came from our house, or from our neighbors.

When I was born, I was one of 9410 people who lived in Williamson. The population didn't include East Williamson and West Williamson, which were outside the city limits, and South Williamson, which was in Kentucky. We were, as the Chamber  of Commerce said, in the "Heart of the Billion Dollar Coal Field." A billion dollars! That must have been all the money in the world. To prove our importance and uniqueness, the Chamber of Commerce had their own building, right next to the Mingo County Court House. It was the world's only building constructed of coal. Bituminous coal.

The Norfolk and Western Railway main line came through Williamson. All during the war, troop trains came through the town a half a dozen times a day, on their way from the Great Lakes Naval Training Station in Chicago to Norfolk, Virginia. The Williamson train station—the depot—was right across from Bassett's Confectionary Store. We boys ran to greet the trains, to wave at the sailors, and to beg for their sailor's hats.

But the coal building and the railroad yards weren't our only claim to fame. We also had the world's largest broom handle factory. We were very important; no wonder we worried about being bombed by the Germans.

Williamson had its own radio station, WBTH, with the station's call letters famously standing for "Williamson Between Three Hills." Our station came on line in 1939 and was affiliated with the Mutual Broadcasting System. It was a new window on the world but not the only radio station we could listen to. My father had purchased a large floor model Zenith radio, which had FM as well as AM and a 78-rpm record player.

The Zenith, an advanced model, whose tubes were considerably smaller than those of the previous decade, was very sensitive and powerful. I listened regularly to WLW, Cincinnati's all powerful 50,000 watt station—"The Nation's Station." I listened to cities too distant to ever dream of visiting: St. Louis, Atlanta, Chicago, and Des Moines, Iowa. I fell asleep many nights listening to the program "Moon River." I learned the words to the opening of the show, the words read by a smooth, deep-voiced announcer, accompanied by the "Moon River" organ:

> *Moon River . . .*
> *A lazy stream of dreams,*
> *Where vain desires forget themselves*
> *In the loveliness of sleep*

> *Moon River . . .*
> *Enchanted white ribbon*
> *Twined in the hair of night*
> *Where nothing is but sleep.*

> *Dream on . . . sleep on . . .*
> *Care will not seek for thee.*
> *Float on . . . drift on . . .*
> *Moon River, to the sea.*

The radio was very important in my young life. My imagination was stirred by such shows as "The Lone Ranger," "Ozzie and Harriet," "The Jack Benny Show," "Bob Hope," "The Fred Allen Show," "Abbott and Costello," "Fibber McGee and Molly," "Edgar Bergen & Charlie McCarthy," and "The Shadow."

My infatuation with radio may have changed the direction of my life. I went to college to major in "Radio Speech"; I wanted to speak into a microphone and have my voice heard a thousand miles away.

Even with the radio expanding our horizons, one could feel claustrophobic in Williamson. The highways were merely paved-over trails. Traveling out of town meant dealing with endless curves on roads that were never level and never straight. The Tug Fork River—which flows down to the Levisa Fork at Louisa, Kentucky to form the Big Sandy River—was navigable only by a rowboat. Air service was an unknown.

But if one wished to see beyond the city between three hills, they could climb to Death Rock. And we boys did that, and from Death Rock we could see mountain range beyond mountain range. In our imaginations we could see the distant cities we could hear on the radio. And from our perch on Death Rock, we could see our great little city and feel happy that the Germans did not come to bomb us.

GOING UP THE STREET

"Hey, Mom, I'm going up the street." I always made sure she heard me, but didn't wait for the obligatory "where are you going?' Up the street could be a block away or more but it was literally up, because there was little flat ground in Williamson. Growing up in a small town in the depression years was a safe environment, and parents didn't worry as parents do today.

There was no shortage of kids to play with. "Kick the Can" was a favorite game. One person protected home plate while everyone else hid. Those hiding tried to reach home plate to kick the can before the defender could tag him. The cans used were rescued from a mother's kitchen.

Football, for little tykes, could be played in a backyard hardly bigger than a good-sized garden. I was tackled once, falling stomach-first on a flowerpot, which banished all the air in my body. I didn't cry because it takes air in your lungs to cry. By the time I could breathe again, I was happy to be alive.

The empty lot adjacent to the church on 6th avenue was a favorite field for our games, but it was also used as a dumping ground for trash. I still sport the scar on my knee that was cut by a piece of glass when I fell. Someone ran to tell my father, and he came to carry me to the hospital. Walking to the hospital meant climbing many steps, and carrying even a child would be difficult. I was about seven and my dad 52. When my father suffered a mild "heart attack" sometime after this incident, it was said that my wounded knee was the cause.

Kids are inventive and adaptable and we had no trouble in finding things to do or places to play. Baseball was played in the streets, with time outs for passing cars. In winter, sledding was a natural for sloping streets. And sometimes the city cooperated by closing streets so we could sled for three blocks without having to stop at an intersection.

As we got older we walked to the high school football field which was a level spot bulldozed from the side of the mountains. Football was played but we had variations depending on the number of boys.

I now find it interesting that we played only with boys; there were never girls in our group. We had no idea how they played, and we never thought about it. Girls had their dolls and stuff, and we had our ball games and stuff. We boys had cars to dream about. Every fall, when the new Chevrolet models would come to be displayed, the boys would rush to the dealership to be inspired by the new lines, or disappointed because the new looked too much like the old. Whatever I thought on that viewing day was forgotten by the next morning; it was not very important or exciting to me.

What did excite me, however, were the long, sleek, and powerful Norfolk & Western 1200-series locomotives that pulled the very long coal trains, sometimes with as many 150

 coal hopper cars. From our house, less than 100 yards from the tracks, we had a perfect view, looking down Dickinson Street, seeing the trains pass. As there was a slight rise in the tracks at this point, the locomotive, straining mightily to gain speed, spun its steel wheels, causing sparks to fly and smoke to belch from its coal-fired furnace.

The N&W proudly announced that a new locomotive had been designed and built to pull their most important passenger train, The Powhatan Arrow. It was anticipated more by not only our gang of boys, but by all our dads and uncles, too. It was anticipated more than the arrival of Santa Claus, and with sheets of steel giving the face of the engine an angular look, it did not disappoint.

The roaring, throbbing sounds of the trains became part of the fabric of living in our town. The train whistles were welcomed, and sometimes the engineer would toot in acknowledgement of the boys who were waving.

In my house, in my makeshift bedroom, 100 yards from the tracks, with the windows open, those powerful coal-fueled, fire-spewing, smoke-belching 1200-series steam-engines caused the doors on my closet to swing open and back. It is how I would fall asleep.

The one time I did not shout to my Mom that I was "going up the street" was when, in a fit of pique for being denied a privilege, I ran away from home. I walked along the tracks following the direction taken by the Powhatan Arrow. However, a family acquaintance picked me up and took me home. I was four years old.

POP, POPEYE & ME

I loved my Pop! I never called him Pop to his face. It was always Papa.

The sound of "Papa" was soothing—something about it was warm and reassuring. It was certainly the name a father should have. Some kids called their Pop "father." Wow, how strange! I wonder if they had a good relationship. My best buddy, Sonny Brown, always said "Sir" to his father. Where was the love in that?

I know Papa loved me long before I knew what was meant by love. I have no recollections of being tossed into the air when I was a toddler, or being bounced on his knee, but he surely did that. I do remember he would lift my sister and me up to his face, to rub our cheeks against his beard. We squealed partly in delight but mainly to object to scratchy feeling of the stubble that had grown out since his morning shave.

Pop always closed his Confectionary store at night, staying to mop the linoleum floors three times a week, arriving home well after we all were in bed. Sometimes, Pop took a mid-afternoon siesta by going to the movies, taking me with him. I didn't understand the romance in movies, and I thought Betty Davis was one funny looking lady. Pop dozed through that movie and many more, but it was for him a welcome break from his usual 16-hour workdays.

He had a wonderful hearty laugh, and if I performed for him, his laugh was especially rich. The best part of the afternoon movie was the shorts, and Popeye was our favorite movie short. Pop encouraged me to sing the Popeye song.

"I'm Popeye the sailor man,
I'm Popeye the sailor man,
I'm strong to the 'finich,
Cause I eats me spinach,
I'm Popeye the Sailor Man."

"Toot, Toot!"

Popeye was never able to protect his love, Olive, until he could gobble a can of spinach, causing an instant mushrooming of his biceps. Only then Olive's rescue was assured.

When I sang Popeye's song, I would flex my muscles, but strangely, nothing happened. There were no muscles in that skinny arm, and my Papa would break into peals of laughter. I was happy because I pleased my father. We did that routine time and time again, always ending up with loads of laughter.

He was my first audience and my first introduction to a life in the theatre.

CLOUDS OF SMOKE

Because my Papa loved me, he was extraordinarily gentle when he confronted my misdeeds.

Pop was a smoker. Cigarettes were always around the house, and cigars, too. A box of cigars sat on the table in the piano room, and I walked by that cache of tobacco for years before, one day, I stopped to study them. A full box contained 50 cigars, and on the day of my misdeed, thirteen had been consumed. It was easy to see that one less cigar would not be noticed. And so it was appropriated.

Bright enough at age nine to know I shouldn't experiment in or near the house, I walked toward town, stopping at the Piggly Wiggly on 4th Avenue. One of the old entrances to the store had been taken out of use. The alcove made a perfect place to get out of the wind and to be hidden from view.

Biting off the end of the cigar, as my Pop did, was a necessary but not pleasant act. The taste of cigar tobacco in my mouth made my saliva flow. Spitting was another part of the ritual. Finally, the match was struck and the flame, applied to the end of the cigar, produced a large blaze and scads of smoke. One puff, two puffs, three puffs in quick succession and the alcove was filled with smoke.

Proud of my deed, I turned to leave taking one short step before abruptly stopping.

I recognized the shoes.

There before me, looking down was Papa. His face gave no hint of his thoughts, or worse, his upcoming actions. It was a glum moment indeed, but without stopping to analyze the situation any further, I flipped the cigar past him into the street gutter.

"I was just trying it out, Papa," I said as brightly as I could, "I wanted to see what it was like."

The pause that followed was neither long nor threatening before the words came out.

"Son, you can smoke if you want to, but I ask you not to smoke before you are 21 years old."

"Okay, Pop, I won't," I blurted out, thankful for the reprieve.

And I meant it. I had no intention of smoking, because I had had my one-puff fling.

"Good!" he said, and put his arm around my shoulder. And we walked home.

PAPA WAS A PSYCHOLOGIST

Each year at Labor Day weekend, the family piled into our Chevrolet sedan for the trip to Huntington or Charleston or Beckley for the annual Kfeirian Reunion. My Papa had been instrumental in starting the reunion of descendants of Kfeir, Lebanon. In Williamson, there were nearly 20 families and more than a hundred each in the other cities. Most of the Kfeirians were related to each other, and so it was appropriate, if you wished, to greet any person with "Cousin," or "Uncle," or "Aunt."

The reunion provided an opportunity to see friends and relatives not seen since last year, and importantly, a chance for young people to meet eligible mates. But for the younger persons like myself, it was a chance to run up and down hotel halls and empty ballrooms.

There was a special chair near the registration desk, and if any person dared to sit in it, they received a surprise, which brought roars of laughter from those nearby. The chair had been wired, and an electrical shock awaited whoever had forgotten about the existence of the chair from the previous year.

. . . . .

One year, several of us boys discovered the game of "elevator operator." It was as simple as pushing buttons. Guests were using the elevator to reach their rooms and we were only too happy to help them by playing elevator operator.

After several successful trips, one trip proved eventful. Somehow, the elevator stuck between floors. We had no idea how it happened or what to do about it. After a few minutes of

slight panic on the part of some passengers and great panic on the part of the boy operators, the elevator started moving and the passengers reached their destination.

Knowing that enough was enough, it was time to leave our plaything and find something new. I thought it would be better for my physical health if I could avoid seeing Papa in the near future. But eventually we met. I expected the worst. But my dad gave me the greatest surprise in my young life.

"Son, I heard how the elevator became stuck and how you got it going again. I am proud of you." Considering myself lucky over-shadowed any feelings of pride I might have had. And with a couple of slaps on the back, we were off on our separate paths.

Years later, after I had learned the concept of "reverse psychology," did it occur to me that perhaps this was Papa's way to say it is better to be a solution to a problem than the cause of a problem.

PAYING COMPLIMENTS

Papa was good at complimenting me, even if it was for effort more than quality. One such compliment filled me with great pride encouraging me to be a hard worker.

Williamson, being at the heart of West Virginia's "Billion Dollar Coal Field," was also an important railroad town. Long trains of coal cars left the rail yards every hour, pulled by powerful coal-burning locomotives. The women suffered the task of scrubbing black rings from around the collars of their husband's white shirts. Coal dust filled the air. Many people suffered postnasal drips, asthma or other respiratory ailments.

The inside of a house was also subject to the effects of coal dust. In our house, after a few years, our wallpaper turned dark. Wallpaper cleaner was the solution. It came in the form of putty. Roll the putty into a ball, and pull it across the wallpaper. Like magic the dirt disappeared.

After a few pulls, it was necessary to knead the putty so that the dirt fell below the surface. One small strip at a time, followed by another and another, and soon progress was substantial. If a person was steady, great sections of the wallpaper could be cleaned. I started working in the stairwell and was too short to reach to the top of the wall. But I went as far as I could.

When Papa came home and saw what I had done, his face and his voice made it clear that I had pleased him. He slapped me on my back and thanked me for work well done. I had done my best.

As I look back, it occurs to me that I probably did not do a good job. I might have even made the staircase splotchy and unsightly. But not another word was said, and I was filled with pride for helping my father.

. . . . .

Another compliment came when I was watching Papa fix a pinball machine.

Papa, the entrepreneur, exploited new ways to make his confectionary store more profitable. He once added a pinball machine, which was very popular with the teen boys and other young adults. They learned to jar the table at the appropriate time to make the ball slither off to the right or left; at least they thought they were influencing the direction of the steel ball.

On occasion the machine quit functioning, and it was my father's job to be the mechanic: find the problem and apply the solution. Whenever he opened the machine exposing the inner workings, I was there to watch.

After a particularly perplexing problem I pointed to a device and said, "Fix that, Papa."

And he did!

And the machine worked!

Of course, I had no idea what the device I pointed to did. But Papa slapped me on the back and gave me a smile before announcing widely to everyone in the store that I had fixed the pen ball machine.

Wow! Was I proud!

DRIVING WITH PAPA

I was nearly six years old when my father bought our first family automobile. It was a green 1936 Chevrolet four-door sedan. He was 50 years old, and as far as I know, had never before owned or even driven a car.

While automobiles provided great convenience, they were not the most comfortable mode of travel for a young person with a sensitive stomach. Cars at this time were built high off the ground, causing them to sway around corners and bounce on rough pavement.

A frequent trip for my family was from Williamson to Pikeville, to visit with my mother's brothers and their families. The two-lane highway US Route 119 snaked its torturous way up and down the Appalachian Mountains of Eastern Kentucky. If roads could talk, this road would ask, "what do you mean 'straight'?"

As we curved around the mountains, I would study the route and wonder why the road did not go on the other side of the valley where it would have been less curvy. "If only," I  thought to myself, "they would build a bridge from this point to that point, we could go in a straight line. We could get there faster and I wouldn't get sick." But the roads in this part of the world had never been improved since the first pioneers drove their mule trains from here to there.

To keep my youngest sister Lorraine and me from becoming car sick, which we did regularly on these trips, my mother learned that lemon juice would quell our stomachs.

"Suck on this lemon" she would instruct, giving one half to me and the other half to my sister.

It worked. We learned to travel the 30-mile trip, which took one and one-half hours, without demanding that the car be stopped before we threw up the contents of our stomachs.

One unintended consequence was that I became addicted to lemon, and to this day I love to eat salads and vegetables flavored by quantities of lemon juice.

When Papa bought the Chevy, the four oldest girls in the family were teenagers and had their own lives to lead. It was Lorraine, and I, the two youngest, who would be taken on trips to visit relatives. Once during road construction, instead of following in convoy style, and suffering the dust that blew into windows, Papa started passing cars. We were stopped by the convoy police and given a warning to stay in line.

We had Bassett cousins in Welch, West Virginia, and the road to Welch, US 52, was good in spots, including a deep cut through a mountain ridge that saved minutes in travel time. This section of the highway actually had a concrete pavement. After one such visit to Welch, we encountered thick fog on our return home. Sitting in the back seat, I studied the road intently, but fruitlessly, to see where Papa was taking us. Finally, unable to see anything and sure that we would be killed, I threw myself on the floor behind the front seats and fell asleep. It was a welcome surprise to hear my mother tell me to wake up and go to bed.

Papa's mother Miriam lived on the farm just north of Blissfield, Michigan, and in the summer we made trips north to visit. The first trip was the most memorable. Coming from hilly West Virginia and moving through northwest Ohio, we came upon roads that were straight for as far as one could see. I would turn and look out the back window discovering that the road to the South was just as straight as the road to the North.

Imagine, from horizon to horizon a straight road. Why, one could ride for hours and not suffer motion sickness!

Owning an automobile gave rise to travel plans. In the late 1930s papa announced that we were going to take a vacation at Virginia Beach. It would have been my first visit to see an ocean. My great excitement for this trip was only exceeded by my greater disappointment when I heard later that the trip had been cancelled.

In the 1930s, my sister Selma was enrolled at Berea College in Kentucky and sister Alice was at Concord College in West Virginia. We traveled to both locations, and both trips were memorable. I saw my first squirrels in Berea. Driving to Concord from Beckley, the road had been built on the ridges, allowing one to look out over the West Virginia mountains. In Williamson, one could only look up to the mountains.

In 1942, Papa was in an automobile accident, the details of which were never talked about. Apparently, he was traveling alone, to a site in Mingo County where he had placed some slot machines. After the car was towed to the Chevrolet dealership, I went to inspect the damage. There were deep dents and bumps on all sides of the car, and the windshield was broken, suggesting that the car had been rolled. Papa escaped without major physical injury, but he had a nasty cut on the shin of his right leg, a wound that took months to heal. In time the car was repaired and returned to service.

Like all boys, I wanted desperately to drive a car. I must have been persistent to the point of being a terrible pest, because one day my dad stopped the car in a quiet neighborhood and told me to get behind the wheel. Without any instructions on shifting the gears, he told me to drive. I failed, and I was quieted for the time being, but not for very long. A year later, at a picnic ground, with Papa's encouragement, I moved the car up a short steep grade, spinning the wheels to start the car moving. Pop applauded the effort and the result.

I can recall my first experience in driving on the narrow streets of East Williamson, and how relieved I was to successfully guide the auto between the parked cars on my right and the oncoming traffic on the left.

In 1946, when we had moved to Columbus, Papa bought a new, white, four-door Ford sedan. By this time when I accompanied him on trips, he would have me drive, not only to give me experience, but more importantly to allow him to rest. For Papa, driving on short trips to see family and friends was an important form of relaxation. He was 61 years old and still working very hard.

One winter day we were driving on the brick streets in what is now Italian Village in Columbus. Coming to an intersection, I engaged the brakes to allow a car entering the intersection to pass, but the road was frosty and our car began skidding. Most fortunately, the car came to a stop just inches from the other car and what seemed a surefire collision was avoided.

In 1947, Papa and Mama took a two-week Florida vacation, the only time they had been away from home without children. They returned home tanned and relaxed and like all travelers, happy to be home.

In 1948, Papa bought another car, a Hudson, which was as sleek and aerodynamic as an airplane. Passengers stepped down into their seats. It was the last car Papa bought. I remember it because he and Mama, in January 1949, drove to Bowling Green State University to see me. It was a surprise visit. Mama brought my clean laundry and we went out to eat, even though she had also brought food she had cooked. Papa died in March of that year.

A SUMMER ON THE FARM

Knowing now how 14-year-old boys can be difficult, my parents were probably very happy to have me spend the summer of 1945 on my Uncle's Sam's farm near Blissfield,

Mama Rahija, Sitti, Mariam, and cousin Joe

Michigan. When suggested, I was very happy to say yes. I think my Uncle Sam and Aunt Flora were glad to have me, but my grandmother, Sitti Mariam, aged 82, was especially glad. Also, I always got along well with my first cousin, Joseph, 17 months my junior. I looked forward to this new adventure. My family had often made trips to the farm, but we hardly ever stayed more than two nights.

Uncle Sam, my father's brother, expected me to be a member of the family and that meant sharing the work. So when it was time to put up the hay, I had my own pitchfork to lift the hay to the wagon. I learned how the chaff that falls off the fork comes down to lay between your shirt and your skin and how that itches. I got the opportunity to drive the tractor, and that was heady stuff for a youngster. I slopped the pigs, collected the chicken eggs, and shelled the corn.

When the time came, Uncle Sam gave me the opportunity to shoot his shotgun. There was a minimal amount of instruction. I lay the butt of the gun against my shoulder and squeezed the trigger. The gun's noisy blast was anticipated, but not the shotgun's recoil. My shoulder was sore for several days because

I had not held the gunstock firmly to my body. Lesson learned. That was the end of that summer's one-shot shooting adventure.

Boys being boys, I challenged Joseph to jump from the barn's upper loft onto the hay that was lying on the ground. The loft was quite a way above the ground. He said he would do it if I would take a bite of a hot pepper. Okay, I said, and the wager was on. Joe went first and successfully made the leap. When my turn came, I bit into the pepper and immediately knew that I had lost the bet. A gallon of water did not cool my mouth, and rubbing the tongue with my shirt was equally of no value.

On more than one occasion Uncle Sam invited me to accompany him to a farmer's market in Detroit. This was the opportunity for a small farmer to trade farm products for cash. Tomatoes, onions, lettuce, cabbage, corn, and broccoli—whatever was in season—were staples, as were the fresh eggs we had gathered that morning. The produce was, what we would say today, organic. The only fertilizer used was cow's manure for the corn and beans that grew in the field. The garden plot next to the house was unfertilized and grown without pesticide. It was a treat to pick and eat tomatoes unwashed with water but wiped on your shirt, and seasoned with a pinch of salt.

August 6, 1945 was a memorable day as we heard the news that a strange new super weapon was dropped on a city in Japan. It was a nuclear bomb, which was something we did not understand. We listened to the news that day and the next days until the Japanese surrender on August 15. We were happy because we knew many persons who were in the Armed Forces who would soon be coming home.

And coming home is what I did as it was soon time to say goodbye to West Virginia and start school in a new city in Ohio. My summer on the Michigan farm was memorable.

I loved that my Papa's farm family was now my farm family.

CALIFORNIA, HERE I GUN!

I am not sure when I first fell in love with California. It must have been when my sister Alice ("an Eastern Lass" said the headline in the Redwood City Times) met and wed Jack Rutherdale in 1946 and moved west. Her frequent and informative letters painted an idealized picture of life in the "Land Of Golden Hills and Cloudless Skies." Or perhaps I was attracted by the allure of Hollywood or the Pacific Ocean or simply the great distance from Ohio.

My love soon transferred itself into a desire to travel to California. I had, no doubt, an innate sense of adventure. After all, I was sixteen years old—nearly a man—old enough to fend for myself.

"Papa, I want to go visit Alice this coming summer," I said during my junior year in high school. The response from a wise parent was a mild "okay" knowing that September wishes often fade long before the point of no return arrives.

I began telling my friends at school that I was going to spend the summer in California. As spring approached, some doubts about traveling alone and such a long way from home caused a second thought. But the reality of returning to school in the fall and having to explain my non-California adventure would have been too embarrassing. What was I to say? "Oh, I became nervous about traveling and decided I would rather stay home." Or, "My mother really needed me to stay home to cut the grass."

When the time came, Papa said he would withdraw money from my savings account, which I didn't know I had. Nearly $200 had been given in my name when I was born. This was an amazing amount of money for a sixth child born in the height of the depression, but I was my parent's first son after five daughters. My father was 45 years old when I was born and my mother was 39. "Thank God. They had a boy. Now they can stop having children," the donors must have said.

If my father had any doubts or fears about my traveling alone, they would have been tempered by his leaving his home at 16 to start a new life in America. If my mother worried, she would have remembered that she left home at 20, arriving in the land of the free unable to speak a word of English. I was unaware of any trepidation my parents may have had. I had their blessings.

Train travel would have been exciting and fast but expensive. Greyhound was not as fast but still a little expensive. A private automobile might be the least expensive way to travel. I began studying the Columbus Dispatch classified section for announcements of people driving to California who desired a rider to share the expense. In a few days, I found a great prospect. The cost would be only $35. We agreed on the details and on the day and hour of departure.

There were four of us in the car: besides me, there were two women, one a paying passenger, and the driver's six-year-old daughter. We left Columbus early on a June morning heading west on US 40, the Lincoln Highway, heading for Indianapolis and St. Louis. I followed our progress on my map, noting every town and the distance to the next town. It was my first visit to Indianapolis, and Illinois, and my heart pounded as we crossed the great and mighty Mississippi river.

We were on the outskirts of St. Louis when I became aware we were driving on US Route 66.

"You've taken the wrong road", I said, "We should be on US 40."

"Oh, no," she replied. "66 takes us to Los Angeles!"

"But I am going to San Francisco."

The discussion took us nowhere, and I slumped into my seat and stared at the passing utility poles as I contemplated my dilemma. Talk among the others resumed. The six-year old clamoring for attention frequently interrupted the constant chattering of the two women.

"Mommy, are we there yet?" was a refrain that had started before we had left Ohio. "Mommy, I have to go to the bathroom." "Mommy, I am hungry." Her voice was like fingernails on a chalkboard.

"Oh, my lord," I thought, "how would I survive the ride all the way to California?" Surely, the child would fall asleep at night, and the two ladies would be more silent, and peace and quiet would come to me at some time during the night drive.

Approaching Rolla, Missouri, the driver slowed down before pulling into a motel. I was shocked!

"Why are we stopping here?" I cried!

"Well, we are staying here tonight. What are you going to do?" she asked.

Do? It had never occurred to me that we would be staying in motels at night. I thought we would be driving straight through. Adding the expense of a nightly motel room would devastate my budget, and it would extend the trip by several days, during which time my ears and mind would be numb with the idle chattering of the two women and the whiny haranguing of the six-year-old.

I was distraught. My careful plans were not so careful after all. I could have slept in the car but the driver said that would not be possible. I could sleep under a tree but I had no blanket or sleeping bag. I could stay up all night, but I needed my sleep.

I walked into the restaurant, which was adjacent to the motel. There was a U-shaped counter, and I sat at the bottom of the U with my back to the door. My shoulders were drooping and my chin rested on my chest. I was oblivious to the other customers in the café, one of whom was the motel owner who had overheard my arguments with the driver.

At that moment I spied a revolver on a shelf of the U-shaped counter. Sitting up, I began considering my options. I needed to have my $35 returned, feeling that I had been misled. I could take the gun and force the driver to return my money. Time passed as I continued to contemplate my fate. Was the gun my way to California? I went over the options again and again, trying to make sense of what to do.

The motel owner, who had been observing the rising tension, came forward. With soothing tones he suggested a compromise to the driver, who was increasingly aware she had a problem passenger. If I would pay a reasonable amount for the share of the trip from Columbus to Rolla, would the driver return the remaining fare? With the help of our wise moderator and counselor, we quickly agreed that I would pay ten dollars and the driver would return $25. The deal was done and the great weight that stuck me to the ground flew away.

I gathered my suitcase and briskly walked the half-mile to the grocery story that doubled as a Greyhound bus station. I was soon on my way to San Francisco, by way of Los Angeles, riding and sleeping through the night.

In later years, I was haunted by the Rolla experience. What if I had picked up that gun? What if it had been loaded? What if I had accidentally discharged the gun? What if I had wounded someone? What if I had killed a person?

What kept me from reaching for a gun that may have solved a great problem for a sixteen-year-old boy—not yet a man—but created far greater problems? Was it fear, good luck, the intervention of a stranger, or providence that kept my life from taking an awful fork in the road?

Or was it the presence of my father in my heart?

A ROSE BY ANY OTHER NAME

What's in a name?" you ask. Let me tell you.
My father was Pop or Papa to me but to others it could
be A. J., Abraham, Brahim, Abe, and Uncle Abe. My mother
was only Mom or Mamma to her children, but to her friends
she was Rahija. Two of my sisters, Wadad and Alice, had no
special monikers, but Selma was Sally, Lorraine was Lo, or
Loh-RAIN, mimicking the southern West Virginia hillbilly
twain. My oldest sister Gladys was Gladie, or just between the
two of us, Glad-Ass, which became "Happy Bottom." Saying
that moniker was always a cause for Gladys and I to laugh.

As a child, I joked with my father that my name was
"Abra- with a Ham" tied on. He always laughed. I grew up in
the family as Junior, or as I heard it pronounced with strident
hillbilly nasality—JUNE-YER. The older I became the more
the sound grated. When we moved to Columbus (Ohio) in the
summer of 1946, I announced to my family that my name was
Abe and that I would not respond were I to be addressed as
Junior. "Junior is not a name; it does not identify who I am," I
announced. It took two weeks of training, but the family came
around and my name became Abe.

In high school, college, and the United States Army, I was
officially Abraham Joseph Bassett, Jr., but Abe to friends.
When Papa died in 1949, I dropped any occasional use of the
Jr. As I recall, Papa seldom if ever used the title of Sr.

After I discovered that Abe Bassett contains five pairs of
letters: A - B - E - S - T, I playfully asserted that I am "Sabet
Sabet" or "Sabet2." I am so identified in my high school annual.

When I received my Ph.D. diploma, I refused to accept

it until my name was changed to Abe J. Bassett. That is my official name for all legal purposes: Passport, Social Security, financials, licenses, etc.

In my lifetime, people have used the following monikers for me: Junior, Abraham, Brahim, Abe, Abie, Abie Joe, Yussef, A. J., Dad, Unkabe (pronounced oon-KAH-bay) and Uncle Abe. My son Douglas decided he would call his parents by their first name even though our letters to him were always signed Dad and Mom. The most laughable name is "Nano Baby," invested in me by Stella, my nearly 3-year old Italian granddaughter. Her sisters had called me Nano Abie. (Nano is grandfather in Italian.)

Abraham is an uncommon name in the 20th century but was widely used in the 19th. I found many persons named Abraham Bassett who migrated from Britain. Admiration of Abraham Lincoln may have been a cause of the greater use of the name. I think a reason for the demise of Abraham as a first name is that it tends to identify a person as an Arab, a Jew, or a Muslim, or even as a religiously conservative person. It is clearly out of fashion these days.

I have grown to see the advantage of owning a distinctive name. If you Google "Abe Bassett," "White Pages" will tell you there is only one person in the United States with that name. Some search engines will say there are two, but that would include Abe N. Bassett of Oak Harbor, Ohio and Sun City, Florida. He is a second cousin, now deceased.

A Google search will also lead to the Wright State University Libraries CORE collection where you may hear me being interviewed, read that interview, or read my article on artistic censorship. On that site is also *Memories of Rahija*, the public domain book about my Mother.

So what is in a name? Everything! Including roses!

II | *REMEMBERING MAMA AND PAPA*

THE DEATH OF PAPA

It was hard to accept the death of my Papa. I was only 18 at the time and my father, age 63, was supposed to live forever. We didn't have the conversations we should have had, but would have had if only he had waited a while. He didn't have a chance to share more of his wisdom with me. We weren't able to say goodbye.

I cherish the surprise visit from my parents six weeks earlier, when they came to the university I was attending to deliver clean clothes, to take me to dinner, and to spend a few hours with their only son.

It was the second semester of my freshman year at Bowling Green when I received a telephone call from my sister Lorraine. Papa is sick, she said, and I should come home. Not understanding the gravity of the situation I said I could come tomorrow after an exam, but she pressed me to return as quickly as I could. I recall the journey home, which I did by hitchhiking, and having the worried feeling that my father was indeed sick, perhaps deadly sick.

That was the situation when I entered the house. Papa was sitting in a chair in his bedroom attended by a doctor and surrounded by my mother and some of my sisters. He was unconscious and unresponsive and the doctor's face revealed the severity of the ailment.

Papa had suffered a cerebral hemorrhage as it was called in 1949 and what we would say today was a severe stroke. Papa always had a stocky build and carried excess weight all his life. He and my mother had once gone to the Mayo Clinic, and when they returned Mama cooked a special diet for him. It is clear now that he suffered from excess weight and high blood pressure, much of it a result of a life of rich foods in excessive quantities. Add to that the stress of a lifetime of hard work, the use of tobacco, and with today's hindsight, the results were predictable.

However, I have my own theory as to the cause of the untimely death of my father. The previous November, Papa was working in the tavern installing a large keg of beer in the basement directly underneath the bar. The metal beer keg is under great pressure, and there was a rod in the keg, which during the installation was released with great force, hitting Papa in the cheek. I learned of this severe injury only when I came home for Christmas. I suspect that the hemorrhage was the result of a blood clot that formed and found in time its way into the brain.

Within a few hours of my arrival that afternoon, March 28, 1949, Papa expired. I don't recall a scene of loud crying. I believe we were all in shock. Telephone calls quickly went out to the family and to friends, and a date for the funeral was set.

Uncle Frank was summoned from Detroit, and I was sent the next day to pick him up at the train station, along with my brother-in-law Bill Scott, and one other person. No one spoke a word as we rode from the station to the house. When the car stopped and everyone got out, Uncle Frank still had not been told of the situation. It was left to me to say that Papa was dead. By this time the gravity of the situation must have been obvious, but still he needed to be told before he came into the house. That instant was perhaps the most serious moment of my life, and only as I look back do I see it was a turning point from adolescent toward adulthood.

Papa was beloved by all his friends and acquaintances. Funeral services were held at Trinity Episcopal Church in downtown Columbus, and the church was filled to capacity. The number of automobiles parked in Broad Street beside the church was four rows deep. Mama was devastated, and I have the vivid image of walking her out of the church with my arm around her shoulder. I recall thinking that I did not want to be here. I didn't want this responsibility. But there I was, an eighteen-year-old standing in for my father, a prop for my mother.

Hundreds of people came back to our house, where women had prepared food. I was surprised to learn how hungry I was and what a relief it was to have the burial over. One high school classmate, Jim Barnes, came to the house to offer his condolences, and that was an act of kindness that I have never forgotten. Many other classmates would have come but most of them were out of town attending college.

My sister Lorraine has vivid memories of older persons traveling to Columbus for the funeral. She recalls the sobs of our Aunt Hiceebe, and the anguish of the elderly George Cantees. Papa's sudden and untimely death was a shock for many life-long friends and cousins who truly loved and respected Abraham Bassett.

I returned to the university and finished my studies for the year, completing what was a mediocre first year in college. That summer, I traveled with Bill Scott to California where we visited and stayed with my dear sister Alice and her husband, Jack Rutherdale.

When school resumed in September I had no notion that I was a different person, but from that time on I was a serious student. My grades, and this is in the days before the so-called "grade-inflation," were always above a 3.25 average. I was very active in extracurricular activities and in working. I never thought that this improvement had anything to do with the death of my father, but now I do. It was time to grow up and take responsibility for myself because no one else would be there to take care of me.

I think of Papa often, and wish I could bring him back for a 30-minute conversation. My feelings for him are very warm when I look at his photographs. His look is so familiar, but sometimes I think I don't know him. I can't remember his voice, but I do recall the smell of his suits because he was a smoker.

I know that Papa loved me. Papa was 45 and Mama was 39 when I was born, and they had worked very hard to raise their family of six children. I was the baby and only son. By the time I was born, they had become wise parents. We lived in a safe city and times were safe. There was no hovering over me, no super directing to guide my every step. And while in the process of learning to become an adult I yearned for more guidance and more direction, I appreciated the love that I always knew my father and mother had for me.

Love is the greatest gift a parent can give a child.

ENCOUNTERS WITH PAPA

I was up exceptionally early this morning, cheating myself on the minimum amount of sleep needed for a fully functioning day. I dressed, fixed coffee, and read the newspaper. Before starting on my scheduled tasks, I thought it better if I took a short nap in my family room recliner, soon falling into a deep, refreshing, 30-minute nap. When the telephone rang, I struggled to get out of the chair and rushed to the phone.

It was then that I realized I had been in the midst of a deep and wonderful dream. I rarely recall dreams, but this was a dream too awesome to forget. Perhaps I should thank the rude and incessant ringing of the telephone.

It was a dream with Papa. As the dream started, Papa was sitting before me. I wondered how could this be, Papa has been gone for more than a half-century? Unable to explain his presence, I decided to spend my energy in conversation, not in speculation. Pop, as I frequently referred to Papa during my teen years, was dressed in a suit and tie, his usual mode of attire. He looked refreshed and relaxed.

"Papa, where did you arrive when you came to America?" I asked.

"I came from Copenhagen," he said clearly, but where he landed was garbled. Did he say Long Island?

"Papa," I asked, "when you came to America with your father, was that the first time he had been to America?" Papa didn't know the answer but he said that his father had six brothers. At this point Papa got up to leave, walking to the elevator.

"Wait, don't go," I said, following him. It was than that the phone rang and I struggled to get out of the chair, and then Pop was gone.

I was so sorry to lose contact, but being with him for even a moment was sweet. Do you suppose he will come back for another visit?

. . . . .

There was a second encounter with Papa and the only one that occurred in daytime.

Interstate highway 675 was under construction near our house. I walked to the site after the workmen had gone home and sat on a large sewer pipe. It was late afternoon. All was quiet.

It was at that time I felt Papa's strong presence. He was there with me. I couldn't see him and we didn't speak but his presence was real. It was warm and sweet.

Papa had come back for just a moment to be with me, to let me know he loved me and that he missed me.

Our souls had touched before he returned to the place he had come from.

MEMORIES OF MAMA

Rahija Jamra Saad Bassett
May 26, 1891 - June 19, 1983

*What follows are memories of my mother that were first published in
Memories of Rahija in 1992. This publication is available through Interlibrary
Loan, and can be read online at the Wright State University Dunbar Library
CORE website.*

Eterna Femina

Mama had a myth she lived by. It was that she and Papa would have a large house on some acreage, and all her children would have their own houses on the same land. We would all be one happy family, and Mama would be forever mother of us all.

A Sad Moment

Mama frequently told the story of how, as a young child of three or four in Kfeir, when she was sick and not feeling well, she asked her mother to wipe her nose. The request earned her a slap across the face.

It always seemed to me that Mama never understood the reason for the rebuke from her mother, but blamed herself.

The story was never told as a story with a moral, but as a sad moment in her life.

Mama Was A Party Girl

Mama could be tired or emotionally down, but whenever there was an upcoming event, she found the energy to cook a special dish, dress up, put on makeup, and go out. It might have been a church service, an Eastern Star meeting, a trip to the store, or a visit at a friend's house.

I often said to her, "Mama, you're a party girl, you love to go out." She never denied it.

All Her Children

I never remember Mama saying a bad thing about any specific person, though I do recall her thinking that certain groups of people were "bad people." For example, people who hurt other people were bad. These "bad people" would earn her most severe disapproval, which was usually a guttural Arabic sound and a sneering lip.

But she never thought ill of anyone. She loved all her children and loved them equally, and she would never entertain the thought that one child was more important than another.

Mama's Long Wash Day

Monday was washday and Tuesday was ironing day when I was a child. All six children lived at home until my sisters started going to college. Until Alice went to college, we were all home during the summer.

The amount of washing to be done was truly prodigious. Laundry was done in the basement, and I recall the two washing machines we owned in Williamson. The first had inverted brass-bowl plungers that pushed the clothes down into the water. A more modern Maytag replaced it with its twisting rotor. There were three tubs that contained rinse water, and each piece of laundry had to be wrung through rubber rollers as it went from one tub to the other.

Sometimes Mama or one of my sisters would get their hands caught in the wringer, and it took a deft move by Mama to hit the safety release lever on top. Once done, the hand could be extracted.

In spite of this modern convenience, Mama had a washboard, which she used occasionally for some stubborn piece of dirty clothing. The heavy baskets of damp clothes were carried outside and hung on lines in the back yard. After the clothes dried they were returned to the basement for ironing.

Tuesday was ironing day, and it was equally long and arduous, even after Papa bought Mama a mangle for shirts and flatware. I was about seven or eight years old and I remember the talk and anticipation about the mangle, and later, the disappointment that this modern labor saving device still required a lot of human toil.

The washing and ironing were done in the basement, and the basement could only be accessed through a trap door in the kitchen floor. The door was too heavy for a boy to lift and the steps too steep for a child to be trusted near. These steps were the path to the clotheslines in the back yard, and they were the steps to the second floor bedrooms, the destination of ironed shirts and sheets, clean towels, and clothing.

Mondays and Tuesdays were always long, long days, and even as a child I seemed to know that Mama had to work very hard on washdays.

Mama the Traveler

Mama had a child-like exuberance for life: she loved to meet new people, see old friends, go to parties, travel, and experience new things. It was only natural that she should come to visit Sharon and me and our children when we lived in Missouri, North Dakota, and Washington.

I particularly remember a ten-day visit to Tacoma. I arranged to have daylong trips balanced with close-to-home activities. There was a trip to Mt. Rainier, then to Olympic Peninsula, and then to the tulip and flower fields in Puyallup, to Olympia and the fish hatchery, and to Seattle.

It was a joy to show the area to Mom because each view of Mt. Rainer or Puget Sound, or each unique flower or new tree, was greeted with wide-eyed delight and joy. She was constantly amazed, enthralled, captivated, by both nature and things man-made. She thoroughly enjoyed every moment of every day on that visit, capping each day's activities by recording the events in her diary.

It made her visit with us joyful and welcome.

A Corset

At times Mama rued her Americanization. She used to lament that when she came to Pikeville they put her in a corset, and she never felt she needed one. As a child, when I was still allowed into Mama's boudoir, I watched her struggling to lace her corset, and I was in full agreement with her lament.

We have a splendid photograph of Mama in a fine embroidered dress with her hand resting on a parasol; a hat finished the portrait of a very elegant and beautiful young lady. I suppose a corset contributed to the straight back.

The Ayn of Kfeir

Mama had a thing for well water.

Whenever we were traveling and Mama spotted a well, be it in the country or in a village, she asked Abraham to stop, which he did without argument. Mama and Papa would take the cup and sample the water, announcing that this was indeed fine water, inviting Lorraine and me to partake.

Once when we were in eastern West Virginia, the well water had a particularly strong sulphurous smell. I couldn't possibly get close enough to the water to taste it; the smell alone repelled me. But Mama took the water, pronounced it fit, and drank heartily.

Part of the attraction must have been the notion that if it tasted bad, it must be good for you. The evidence in that idea was the castor oil they poured down our throats when we complained of being ill.

It was much later in my life that I realized that Mom's love of country wells and water was an important link to the ayn of Kfeir and her childhood home.

A Dress

When I was in Okinawa I purchased several yards of very fine green silk brocade to be made into a dress for Mama. She had the material made into a skirt and jacket and it was a handsome outfit. For the next thirty-five years, she wore this suit for special occasions.

I think she loved this dress because the material was beautiful, the dress was elegant, she looked attractive in the outfit, and her son had purchased the material.

A Free Spirit

After Mama's funeral we had a wonderfully warm and loving remembrance for Mama in the basement of Trinity Episcopal Church in Columbus. We saw slide pictures of Mama and listened to her tape-recorded voice telling her favorite stories.

At the conclusion, Sharon, Corta (my mother-in-law), Douglas, Valerie and I returned to our home in Dayton. When we walked into the family room, there was a sparrow flying around the room. Involuntarily, but immediately, I quietly exclaimed "That's Mama!"

Corta was startled by my comment, but I knew what I knew. We opened the door, allowing the bird to fly away.

A Nose for Vines

Mama had a nose for grape vines.

Whenever she visited me, hardly any time passed before she went for a walk with an empty grocery bag under her arm. In a short while she would return with a bag full of grape leaves. "Mom", I would say, "Where did you get those grape leaves?"

"Oh, down the street at the blue house."

"But, did you ask?"

"Oh, it's okay, they won't mind."

No Swearing Allowed Here

Mama would not allow me to say any "dirty" or "bad" words, which is why I was so shocked about her "swearing".

When she hurt herself, she would shriek out an Arabic phrase, which I knew was swearing, because it sounded like swearing. "*Yihraq `iid-ish-shaytaan!*" she shrieked while I shuddered.

It was only years later that I had the nerve to ask her for a translation, which was, literally, "May the Devils' hand be burned!"

A Practical Joker

Papa was a practical joker and often the joke was at the expense of Mama.

One of the stories she frequently told me was the time Papa came home late at night and came into her room. She awoke with a start when Papa dangled his socks before her nose.

In remembering the story now, it seems to me that Mama told it in mock-horror, mock-disgust, almost admitting she enjoyed sharing Abraham's delight even when it was at her expense.

Learning Arabic

By the time I was in graduate school at Ohio State and living on the third floor of Mama's house, I really wanted to learn Arabic.

"Speak to me in Arabic, Mama," I would implore her, and she would try. But by this time in her life, Mama had difficulty in speaking 100% Arabic. Her speech was truly half-Arabic and half-English. This was demonstrated one day when I knocked on the bathroom door and Mama, who was inside, responded with "*Anii*, Honey" ("It's me, Honey.")

An Endless Garden

Returning from Army service in 1954, I spent the summer in Columbus.

I worked in the Towne Tavern and did maintenance at the house. Cutting the grass in the back yard was a most tedious chore, not only because of the summer heat and the size of the yard, but because it was done with a push-reel mower. Mama must have been appreciative of my work because she would bring me a large glass of lemonade to cool me down and to replace the fluids I had sweated away. I was certainly appreciative of this kindness.

We had no fresh vegetables in Okinawa, and I had an insatiable craving for salads that summer. Mama made me a huge bowl of salad every day, and by mid-summer I was eating tomatoes and onions and cucumbers from her garden. I couldn't get enough, and I loved every bite of it . . . all ten thousand bites of it!

Nostalgia

My sisters and I regret that we couldn't have arranged to have Mama return to Lebanon for a visit. Mama was very nostalgic about her childhood home and yearned deeply to return. She needed, as everyone needs, a chance to contact the early part of her life. She wanted to see her house, to drink at the *ayn*, to walk to the school, to pick a fig or grape, to see a goat or sheep on the hillside, to view *Jabal el Shaykh*, to visit the folks still alive, and to meet their children and grandchildren.

When I was growing up, I thought many times I would like Mama to return for a visit, but I dismissed the thought for the same reason that Mama did. We never thought it possible. She still thought of the trip as a three to four week ordeal; days of walking, days of waiting, days of train rides, a week at sea. The voyage was too difficult and too expensive for us to seriously consider it.

Mama the Musician

I remember Mama as a lover of music.

It wasn't an extraordinary thing that I should have this image of Mama because I grew up with music in the house.

All of my sisters played musical instruments. They played the piano, the mandolin, the cello, the French horn, the clarinet, and the bass tuba. I had drumsticks and a trombone. Mama sang and she played the piano, which she had taught herself to do.

But Mama had a special instrument which she played for me, often on my request. What I called the *duqq or duuq-duuq* ("knock, knock"), was a wooden bowl and mallet used to pulverize seeds, spices, and coffee beans. By beating the mallet first against the bottom and then against the side she created a *darbákki*-like rhythm suitable for the *dábki* or accompaniment of a song.

Mama sang constantly. *Heekií-ni cal-t-alifoón kill yawm marra, kill yawm marra...* ("Speak to me on the telephone, every day, once everyday, once") was one of our favorite songs.

I never failed to delight in her singing, and unlike my own children, never once felt embarrassment at a singing parent. She made it seem that singing was a natural thing to do.

When I starting dating Sharon, it was no small attraction to me that she sang so beautifully. I guess Mama the Musician set it up.

A Dream: Dustin Hoffman Is My Cousin

I am sitting with my mother and Dustin Hoffman at the round table in the corner of the store near a window. On the same side of the room is a tall soda counter and between the table and the counter is a curtained entrance to "the back room."

The store, with its incandescent lights and wooden floors, has a feel of the 1930s. At the table also sits a couple from the Old Country who now live in America. He is a quiet man in his late thirties with an even quieter wife.

My mother sits with her back to the counter, Dustin is in the corner to the right of my mother and I sit at her left. Dustin and I are talking. When I tell him that I have come out of the ethnic closet to take pride in my heritage he reveals that he is one-half Lebanese. He tells me that his childhood home is Lowell, Massachusetts, and when I ask if he knows "Uncle" Mike Bassett, he says he does and that he is a cousin to Mike. I ask if he knows Gerri Deschanes, he replies, "Yes, she, too, is my cousin."

Excited beyond words, I yell and jump up and down. Everyone hears me and comes to see what is happening. I shout, "Dustin Hoffman is my cousin; Dustin Hoffman is my cousin." Someone begins taking group pictures to mark the occasion.

We are eating. Mama has a spinach *fatiiri* on her plate and she tears a corner from the *fatiiri* and gives it to me and it melts in my mouth.

Where is Dustin? I don't know where Dustin is. I want to see Dustin to tell him that I think he is one of America's greatest actors.

I recall the interview he gave to Richard Merriman in *LIFE* Magazine before the release of *Little Big Man*. In that interview, Dustin quotes from Walt Whitman: " . . . out of the nine month midnight . . ." and I want to tell him that I remember that. I want to say that everything he has done has been wonderful: *The Graduate, Little Big Man, Tootsie, Death of a Salesman, Rainman.*

I can't find Dustin: has he gone?

I wake up from my dream to go to the bathroom and my dream is gone, but I am left with good feelings.

It felt good to be with Mama again.

April 19, 1989

Mama Said I Was An Angel

After living ten years out-of-state, we returned to Dayton, Ohio, in 1970. Through the years I was frequently in Columbus on business trips, and always dropped by the house to say hello to Mama either before or after the meeting.

I would walk into the house, usually without knocking or ringing the doorbell. Almost always, Mama was either in the front room watching television or writing in her diary, or in the kitchen cooking.

"Hello, Mom," I would announce, and she would never fail to be surprised, then amazed, and then delighted. She would say, "You are like an angel, who comes from my dreams. I was thinking of you, and here you are!"

And we would laugh together.

III | THE LEARNING YEARS

WHEN DOLLY WAS CLONED

After Dolly, the Dorset sheep, was cloned in Scotland in 1996, the possibility of cloning human beings became a topic of discussion. It was then that I told my wife that I wished to have myself cloned. "Hush," she said, "people will think you are weird if you say that." She didn't ask why I would want to be cloned, so I am going to tell you why.

If I had a clone of myself from birth, I could raise "Junior" perfectly because I would understand him perfectly. I would know his needs and desires and be able to help him develop his capabilities. It is not that I want to develop a superman, just a person able to achieve his potential.

This raises the questions: Who am I? Who and what could I have been? What was missing in my life that I would like to correct? Oh, my, such ponderous questions. Let me answer these fundamental questions in the following manner:

I was a curious child who lacked guidance. Growing up, I had no idea what a lawyer did, how banks made money or how one became a doctor. I don't think I ever heard the word "professor" or hundreds of other professions, such as paleontologist, archeologist, anthropologist, or psychologist.

I was not a reader, and our Williamson library did not have a children's section. While in junior high school I checked out a Tolstoy novel, but became frustrated when I couldn't pronounce the Russian names. It was not until I was in my thirties and a father when I first read a Mother Goose rhyme. Oh, what a wonderful discovery that was, even if it was thirty years late.

A movie (whose title I do not remember) impressed me as a boy because in it, a sophisticated and knowledgeable adult was schooling an Indian lad of 12 in the ways of the world. I wanted to be that child. I was hungry to know more and to be intellectually stimulated and challenged.

Once, while I was sitting in the back of the family car, my sisters were using the word "intelligence" to describe a person they knew.

"What is intelligence," I asked? I didn't quite understand the answer they gave me, but I never forgot the word "intelligence."

Considering that I was born to two immigrant parents who had a limited command of the English language, and that I was born and raised in a small town that many would label as "backwater," it is remarkable that I earned three college degrees, and become a university professor and administrator.

When I look back on the little pushes that led me in that direction, I start with an incident from the first grade. "Look, Papa, look Mama, I can write 'apple—A P P L E." Looking back over my shoulder I saw my father, with his arm around my mother, smiling at my accomplishment. It was a genuine smile. They were both so pleased to see their skinny-armed six-year-old son on his first step toward education.

I looked forward to Mrs. Robinson's spelling bees in the third grade. Somewhere between the third and fourth grade I discovered that I knew the answers to the questions that the teachers asked, and that I might as well get credit for being the first to answer.

In Jr. High School, the students were given a battery of tests, taken in the old swimming pool, which had been floored over to add more instructional space. After the tests were scored, we met with a teacher who gave us feedback on our performance. I don't remember the words used or any specific information about the tests, only the general impression that I had done well on the tests. That impression stuck with me.

The rest of my West Virginia high school career was

without special merit, except I was in the band and took a speech and drama class from Ms. Rose G. Smith, who also taught French. But at the end of my sophomore year, the family moved to Columbus, Ohio, and to the sophisticated upscale suburb of Upper Arlington, with its advanced school system.

Ms. Vera Randall, the senior English teacher, assigned a term paper, which sent me to the Columbus Public Library to do my research on Al Capone. I enjoyed the process of digging through newspaper files to piece together a coherent story. I really did very well on another paper I did for Ms. Randall on how to hitchhike, based on my experience of getting to California the previous summer. Ms. Randall drilled us weekly on vocabulary and by the time we took the Ohio Psychological Exam—essentially a vocabulary test—at the end of the year, we did quite well. I knew I had learned a great deal in her class when I found my college composition class to be easy.

The first of three very significant incidents occurred in my freshman year at Bowling Green State University. Mr. Coffee, my physical education teacher, was a graduate student needing experience in administering IQ tests. I quickly agreed when he asked if he could give me an IQ test. I had never taken the test, and this might answer my youth question "What is Intelligence?" The results were quite startling to Mr. Coffee and to me. With a reported IQ of 141, I was clearly working below my level.

At the end of my freshman year, when I was 18, my father died suddenly. I recall the image of a thin, tall 18-year-old boy with his arms around the stooping shoulders of his mother, leading her out of the church. It was a symbol of my new life: a fatherless boy who had to assume more responsibility, and a student who had to work to his level.

From that moment on, my college career was altered. I became a serious student who worked to achieve his potential.

I loved my college experience. I loved going to class. And I even learned to look forward to examinations, knowing that the main purpose of a test is to force once to review and master the material. I would relive those years if I could, my cloned self or my actual self.

In my senior year, the Dean of the Graduate School approached me, inviting me to take, in my last semester, a graduate class. I respectfully declined, but the gesture was extremely important. The Dean said by this invitation that I was graduate material. Amazing.

As a college teacher of acting, I learned that one of the most important gifts I could give a student was permission: permission to not fear failure, and thus permission to be creative. It is the same gift a loving parent can give a child. Most of us are born with intelligence and creativity, and those of us luckier than others, did not have those attributes stifled. I often asked my acting students to sing a few measures.

"Oh, no, I can't sing," said some of them.

"Why not?"

"My mother said I should never sing . . . and I haven't."

The image of my dad and mom standing behind me, taking pride in my spelling of "apple," has stayed with me all my life. The message of their unintended but meaningful gesture was priceless as it said: "It is good to learn; we are proud of you; we know that your success in life starts with education."

So, yes, I would clone myself so that my cloned son would have heard about paleontology and archeology, psychology and philosophy at an early age. He would have had voice lessons and tap dance lessons, and know how to pronounce Anna Karenina. I would have loved being a father to my cloned son, even if he had turned out to be a she.

HIGH SCHOOL SCHOLAR

If you ask me if I was bored when I was in school, I would have to say no, never. However, I do recall days at Williamson Junior High School, in the spring, with warm breezes blowing in through the windows, and the smell of blossoming trees, my mind drifting to baseball and the St. Louis Cardinals. When I think about it, I was probably bored in my 10th grade Biology class because to this day I can't think of a single thing I learned. Our teacher was a coach who, like his pupils, had a mind that was elsewhere.

My recently re-discovered high school grade cards show how ordinary a student I was. Ordinary? Well, that puts a positive spin on the truth. I was A's and B's in the ninth grade, except for Latin and English, where I passed by the skin of my teeth. It probably didn't hurt that my sister Selma was the Band Director that year and a good friend of Pearle Nelms and Elizabeth Hall, English and Latin teachers respectively.

Williamson High's college prep curriculum required two years of Latin, which I was able to pass only because Miss Hall gave us a weekly vocabulary test. The study of Latin is a cumulative affair, and it is obvious I hadn't accumulated much as the semester progressed. My period grades went from C to D to F. The second semester was hardly better, but somehow, Miss Hall saw fit to give me a D average on period grades of F, F and D plus a D on the final exam. I guess she liked me and probably needed my warm body to fill the class for Latin II in the sophomore year. By the last grading period of the second year my Latin grade had risen to a commendable C, and I received a C for the semester.

Pearle Nelms, the English teacher, was a pert and diminutive red-haired teacher, and that is all I remember about her or my English class. There was a memorable embarrassing moment that occurred a few years earlier. She was in a revue presented at the Cinderella Theatre downtown, playing the part of a gun-slinging cowgirl. In her boots and denim skirt she sat in a low sofa throwing her knees apart with her skirt slipping above her knees. She was quite unaware why the titters of the audience progressed to a loud continuous roar of laughter. She must have imagined it was the way she delivered her last line because for the longest time she made no move to correct her posture.

In some subjects I did reasonably well. That is, I wasn't in any great danger of not passing. Decent grades were earned in Band, Phys. Ed., Civics and Health; that is, in the less challenging and less-academic classes. Algebra and Plane Geometry were enjoyable courses, and my grades were middle of the class. Mr. Floyd taught "Civics" but I have no idea what was taught. Perhaps it was here I learned to sing the West Virginia State Anthem:

> Oh, the West Virginia hills! How majestic and how grand,
> With their summits bathed in glory, Like our Prince Immanuel's Land!
> Is it any wonder then, that my heart with rapture thrills,
> As I stand once more with loved ones, On those West Virginia hills?

Rose G. Smith was the French, Speech and Drama teacher. We never knew what the G stood for but she was always referred to as Rose G. I didn't study French but my sister Lorraine did and she regaled us as she mimicked Rose G pursing her lips to teach how to properly make the French "ooo" sound. I had Rose G for two years, taking Speech I and Speech II, earning a B in the freshman year and an A in the sophomore year. That was my only A that year.

I know we had homework only because my playmate Freddie Michael boasted that when he came home after school, he first did his assignments before coming out to play. I recall no single homework assignment ever in my first ten years. But I do remember playing after school.

My parents never pressured me to excel in school although I was under some pressure because all my sisters were known as good or excellent students. My father thought education was very important but there was never any father-to-son talk about education. He worked long hours and it was my mother who signed the report cards without comment.

I am extremely proud of my father's goal of seeing that his daughters went to college. This was mainly in the 1930s, during the great depression, when college education was rare for most young people, and especially rare for girls. My parents' six children ended up with five bachelor degrees, three masters' degrees and two doctorates. Five of the six children became teachers.

. . . . .

At the end of my sophomore year, my family moved to Columbus, Ohio, where my father bought a house in the upper crust suburb of Upper Arlington. In our neighborhood we lived next door to a professor from The Ohio State University. Across the street was a lawyer, and there was a telephone company executive, and down the street lived John Galbraith, a millionaire who owned the Pittsburgh Pirates. And on our street lived John Bricker, former Ohio Governor and United State Senator and member of the Knights Templar. Oh, boy, we had moved into the upper suburban stratosphere of Upper Arlington society!

However, we had hardly met any of our neighbors that first summer until the day when I was teaching my Uncle Frank to drive our car. When his foot slipped off the brake, but not off the accelerator, the car shot forward through the garage door and through the back wall of the garage. The entire rear wall of the brick garage was pushed out. Uncle Frank was shaken but not hurt, and I was not hurt but horrified.

The good thing about the crash was that all the neighbors came out to see what had happened and we met neighbors we didn't know we had. Papa had no words of reproach for brother or son, he was just thankful neither of us was hurt. I guess it was my fault, but Uncle Frank shouldn't have been so clumsy. And a 15-year old boy shouldn't have been giving a 55-year-old man his first driving lesson.

· · · · ·

Entering the junior year at Upper Arlington High School was a scary event because most of the students there had been together from the first grade. I had a southern West Virginia accent, a pimply face, and an awkward gait. Sadly, no girl came forward to befriend me, and I didn't mind because, being insecure, I was content to gawk and leer. 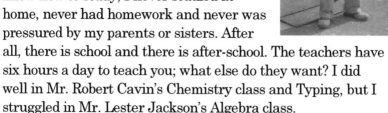 All the girls wore saddle oxfords, makeup, perfume, tight cashmere sweaters, and pearl necklaces; they were as pretty as can be. Many years later during our 50th class reunion, I learned how well they hid their insecurities.

There was more emphasis on schoolwork, much more than I had been exposed to at Williamson. I really didn't know how to study; I never studied at home, never had homework and never was pressured by my parents or sisters. After all, there is school and there is after-school. The teachers have six hours a day to teach you; what else do they want? I did well in Mr. Robert Cavin's Chemistry class and Typing, but I struggled in Mr. Lester Jackson's Algebra class.

Finally, in my senior year, things improved. I had been taken into a fraternity (the "Dracs") and I was adopted by a group of really nice boys. I still ogled the girls without making friends with any of them, except Jo Walker who lived across the street and with whom I would sometimes walk to school.

My grades will not show that my senior English class had a profound influence on me, but it did. Miss Vera Randall—a seeming clone of "Miss Jean Brody"—was tall, unmarried, demanding, devoted to her favorite students, and a good, hard-working teacher. I only earned a C each semester, but I produced my first fictional writing, and my first essays. I accepted her assignments without reservation. For the first time in my life, I worked on my own. I chose Al Capone for the subject of my term paper and spent hours in the Columbus public library reading old newspapers. I actually read a book, Only Yesterday by Frederick Lewis Allen followed by his Since Yesterday to learn the history of the 1920s and 1930s.

Why did I become a student for the first time? What had been missing? Was it in part the educational expectations of the West Virginia community? Or was it because my parents did not threaten or cajole or demand straight A work? Was it because my older sisters did not show the way? Was it because I had never heard a Mother Goose rhyme? Yes, probably all of these things, but mostly because I was immature and unaware. Miss Randall's challenges resonated and moved me.

As I look back on my early years, I remember wondering about the world around me, such as: how do banks make their money; how do people become doctors; what does a lawyer do? But I didn't know how to form the questions and who to ask. My family didn't engage in that kind of conversation. Four of my five sisters became teachers, but as teenagers none of them demonstrated the natural qualities of being a teacher, at least as far as instructing their young brother was concerned.

Perhaps this explains why I would have loved to clone

myself—so I could anticipate and meet the needs of a new little me.

Well, isn't it amazing that with such a poor and slow start in school I graduated from college, and earned two graduate degrees? Did the laissez-faire attitude in which I grew up save me from becoming compulsive, or neurotic? Or was it the love my parents provided that made up for all the other deficiencies? I don't know the answers, but I am happy and thankful that things have worked out so well.

COLLEGE DAYS
1948—1952

While some of my high school classmates attended Ivy League and other private colleges, I enrolled at Bowling Green State University because a course in Radio Speech was offered. I could have attended Ohio State as a good number of classmates did, but I didn't want to live at home. My father or mother did not object, and tuition in 1948 was affordable. In fact, Bowling Green did not have tuition, only fees. And those fees remained steady at $75 per semester for my four years. One of my good friends was ready to enroll at BG with me, but his parents had heard that the students were uncouth and ate with their hands. He subsequently enrolled at Oberlin College.

Radio Speech attracted me because I wanted to work in a radio station. I wanted to broadcast my voice for hundreds of miles. I had no idea what such work would be like or even if a college degree was necessary. Young people at 16 years make decisions based on feelings and wishes, not on reality or facts. My father would rather have me study business so I could work in the family confectionary store, but because I was enthusiastic, he gave his blessing to my dreams.

I lived "on campus" my freshman year. Our "dormitory" was a converted army surplus building, with each room about 12 feet square in which there were two double-deck bunks, two dressers and one desk for four students. The dorm had a "lounge," and it is here where I learned to play pinochle. The dorm was nearly a mile from the main campus, past the city cemetery and adjacent to tomato and cornfields. In the winter, when the northern winds whipped down from the Canadian plains, the walk seemed to stretch for three miles. A good winter coat would have helped insulate my 150-pound no-fat body.

I was not a good student in my freshman year. I wasted much time playing cards, talking with roommates, or doing other non-productive activities. My advisor was Dr. Eldon T. Smith, the department chairman. I told him I would like to take Psychology and Sociology that first semester and was duly enrolled. I was instructed to take beginning English and Spanish. I did well in English because of my excellent high school teacher. The Spanish class was one I passed but without learning anything significant. A no-credit remedial speech class helped rid my speech of its hillbilly accent.

The psychology class, taught by Dr. Myron Fitzwater, became a life-changing experience. We were studying the

question of environment vs. heredity, and at the time, environment was the slight winner. As I thought about this, I reasoned that if environment was more important than heredity, one was not destined from birth to be a certain kind of person. If environment influenced one's behavior and attitudes, than, by golly, I would be able to take charge of my life! I could change bad tendencies or adopt better traits. I reasoned that I was 85% okay, but that I should concentrate on changing 15%. I didn't have anything specific in mind, but I understood that I didn't have to become an expert pinochle player.

I decided to take a second class in psychology the next semester and in fact took one psychology course for each of my eight semesters, making me a de facto psychology major. During my junior year, there were twenty of us in an advanced class, and we sat around tables arrayed in a square configuration. The professor would walk around the room, frequently stopping behind a pretty co-ed with long blond hair. He would touch the hair, feeling its soft texture. He did this on more than one occasion. The girl never reacted, never complained, nor did anyone in class. I was quietly outraged, and I felt sorry for the female student. But this was 1950, and attitudes were what they were.

I took a second class in sociology that freshman year, although I enjoyed the lectures, I decided at the end of the year that sociology is too vague to be of lasting value. I realized that concerns known to sociologists at that time will be outdated in short order. I preferred studies that explain the human psyche or lead us to understand people in the way a class in Psychology or Acting does. In my junior year, I enrolled in Introduction to Philosophy, taught by Dr. Maurice Nielsen. He was a superb teacher whose lectures were well organized and interesting. He made his subject understandable and entertaining by interjecting humorous incidents or interpretations. I finished my undergraduate career by taking a Philosophy course from Dr. Nielsen each semester for two years, ending with a minor in Philosophy.

The other Philosophy classes were Ethics (what is the nature of good?), Logic (what is good thinking?), and the History of Religion. I still have notes from all these classes, and I look at them on occasion. Ethics showed me that the things I wondered about were the things the great philosophers wrote about. Logic taught me logical fallacies, and inductive and deductive reasoning, skills that I used for my entire life. In the religion class we studied all the major religions in chronological order, seeing how each religion was based, in part, on the religion that came before it. I learned how man created religious institutions, often for the benefit of the founders. I was freed of the guilt that religion often places on its adherents, and I was given permission to develop my own understanding of the cosmic questions.

On the day after the last class of my senior year, my classmate and good friend, Howard Ehrenman, and I visited Dr. Nielsen at his home. We presented him with a gift—a record album—saying that we deeply appreciated what he enabled us to learn. The gentle man was embarrassed but pleased because we were genuine in our gratitude.

I had become a serious student at the beginning of my sophomore year. There were four contributing factors to this change: (1) My father had died the previous spring and I had become, so to speak, the man of the family; (2) Psychology 101 had taught me that I had the power to control my life; (3) I no longer lived in an overcrowded and makeshift dormitory; and (4) I developed an interest in theatre.

I was a major in the Department of Speech, which at that time included Radio, Theatre and Speech Correction. I loved all my speech and theatre classes: Public Speaking, Persuasion, Phonetics, Voice and Diction, Acting, and Directing. I worked behind the scenes on many plays. I built sets, did lighting, sound, and stage management. I tried out for parts in plays but acting parts were hard to come by because we younger male students were often competing with World War II veterans.

Being very busy taught me time management. There was no time to waste and little money with which to do time-wasting activities. My grades improved greatly, and I graduated with better than a 3.0 average after a freshman year start of 2.0. My GPA was 3.25 for the last three years, and this in the age before the infamous period of grade inflation. I graduated with 150 semester hours where only120 hours were required for graduation. I think I was seen as a serious student because in my senior year the Dean of the Graduate School invited me to take a graduate course in my final semester. I was flattered but declined to do so. But the invitation set in mind the notion that I was capable of doing graduate work.

Graduate school could not have been further from my thinking when I walked out of my last final examination at the end of my first semester of my freshman year. The relief from pressure, and the resulting feeling of lightness was overwhelming. All tension had dissipated. I floated across the campus. I wasn't aware that finals week could produce such stress, but now I knew. By the beginning of my junior year I came to look forward to test taking. There was no tension. I knew how to study because I had learned how to take good notes and how to prepare for tests. I had come to understand that the purpose of a test is to enable the student to synthesize the material that had been presented during the term. The test had become a vital and welcoming learning experience.

Much of one's learning during college comes not from the courses taken but from fellow students and activities. I sang in the Men's Glee Club my first year and the A Cappella Choir the second year. Here I learned breathing techniques and voice production, which I later imparted to my acting students. Classical music was very important in our lives and I was introduced to mostly romantic symphonies from Tchaikovsky, Grieg, and Rachmaninoff. All students adored the folk singing of Burl Ives, who appeared on the Artist Series.

"Bob," an older student whose last name is forgotten, also influenced me. Years later, I discovered he had been a priest. He lived in a second floor apartment near the city center, equipped with many books and classical music albums. He introduced me to Oscar Wilde's *Reading Gaol* and other poetry. He played music from his abundant classical collection. He discussed philosophical ideas, often taking the contrary point of view to stimulate discussion. Call him a mentor, a tutor, a don; that is what he was, but I didn't know it at the time. His guidance was subtle but significant.

Influence can also come from words chiseled in stone. There was an inscription on the façade of University Library that I read many times over my four years at Bowling Green. "Read not to contradict and confute nor to believe and take for granted but to weigh and consider." (Francis Bacon) I have taken this concept to heart for all these years.

Finally, I learned why graduation is called commencement. It is because we have been set free to begin our life studies. We have been presented with a general framework within which all our new knowledge will be placed. Life is learning and learning becomes life.

IV | LIFE EXPERIENCES

YOU'RE IN THE ARMY NOW
1952-1954

I Steel-toed Boots to Freezing Nights

"**I** swear I am not a communist." "I swear I will wear safety-toe shoes."

With those solemn promises, my well-paying job on the Pennsylvania Railroad was secured for the summer of 1950. This was the summer between my sophomore and junior year in college and I was grateful for the opportunity to return to school with some money in my pocket.

Our days started at 7:00 a.m. with a safety talk. We were warned of the dangers of using the air compressor hoses to bring high-pressure air into any of our body orifices. Since most of the temporary summer help were college students, we thought the safety talks were silly indeed. There were several talks on wearing the steel-toed shoes, in spite of the fact that we were all wearing them. Did they think we were stupid? Was this the army?

Those of us on the lower ranks swept the docks clean, and when one flat car was repaired and moved away, we would pick up rivets and scraps of steel that had fallen to the ground. Our work was mindless and I thought to myself that if I were the boss, I would never pay a person $1.45 an hour to do so little work. Apparently, the yard boss felt the same way; when he received word of an impending inspection by his bosses, we were instructed to get out of sight. We scurried to another part of the gigantic yard and sat in empty boxcars until the all-clear signal was heard.

Our lives changed dramatically on June 25, 1950 when North Korea invaded South Korea. The newspapers were full of Korean Peninsula stories while the United Nations debated the situation. Hour by hour it seemed as if the United States would be involved. As our work was not crucial, we had many hours in which to discuss the war situation. It was fair to say that we were nervous. We had been too young to serve in World War II. We adored those older than we who had fought, but we never thought there would be another war that would involve us.

However, thanks to the Selective Service Systems' student deferment policy, most of us were assured that as long as we stayed in school and progressed to a degree, we would not be drafted. And so it was that as the war raged, we were able to stay in college until graduation.

. . . . .

One of my best friends the summer after college graduation was a high school classmate Bob Parker. When Bob finally got his draft orders, and as I had not, I decided to volunteer so we could go to basic training together. I asked the selective service board to draft me on the same day Bob was called.

Reporting to Fort Hayes in Columbus, we were put through the standard tests and physicals. As I had never had a physical, I was very anxious to learn if I would pass. I wanted to know there were no serious diseases lurking in the recess of my body. We stripped to our shorts at one point and were instructed to turn our head to the right and cough, and then to the left and cough, as a hand jiggled our testicles. This was a test for hernias, or so they said; we joked about other possibilities. Doctors or their assistants looked into our mouths, into our eyes and ears, and we gave a vial or two of blood. We were instructed to go home that first night, but to report the next morning.

It was then that I discovered our plans had been foiled. Bob passed everything, but I flunked the "Wasserman" test.

The Wasserman was a blood test for venereal disease often given as a condition for couples wishing to marry. It had been known for years that the Wasserman, developed in 1923, gave false positive reactions. More blood was drawn, and I was again instructed to return the next morning. Once again there was a positive reading, and more blood was sent to the laboratory. Finally, on the morning of the fourth day, I was deemed to be healthy and was inducted into the army. By this time, however, Bob Parker was in Indiana, as I headed for Virginia. This was not the last time things did not go according to plan.

· · · · ·

"I wanted to be the best soldier I could be," or so I wrote before my enlistment to my sister Alice, herself a World War II veteran. The eight weeks of basic training were very hard, not so much because they were physically tough, but because they were mindless. I quickly saw that the unending drilling had as its purpose the installation in the recruit of an automatic response to a command. Having learned in Psychology 101 about Pavlov and his dogs, I knew I was not likely to "charge" up a hill into torrid sheets of hot flying steel, without such conditioning.

The depression that comes with the onset of basic training does recede in a few weeks, but I was still left with the stupidity of it all, the lack of efficiency, the lack of understanding that some of us actually were capable and wanted to be good soldiers. Of course, the Army was dealing with drafted recruits, most of whom in our training company were uneducated. One young boy had the greatest difficulty remembering his right from his left foot. He regularly incurred the wrath of our First Sergeant who could curse for five minutes without repeating himself. I wanted to laugh, even smile a little, but knew that the slightest twitch at the corner of my mouth would bring the drill sergeant's pretend-wrath and his considerable verbal skills toward me. Basic training was a revelation never before experienced, as I was thrust into a group of so many unintelligent people.

The worst night of my basic training occurred during the "bivouac" in which we went into the cold, damp Virginia woods to do "war games," of which I have few memories. I do remember having an opportunity to throw one live hand grenade. Holding this potentially dangerous weapon in my hand, I pulled the pin that would release the lever that arms the grenade. Knowing it was safe in my hand, I held onto it for an extra second, much to the consternation of my instructor: "THROW IT," he shouted, "God damn it, throw the fucking thing." To relieve his anxiety I threw it, ducked my head behind the sand bags, and waited patiently for the explosion. He thought I was one of the stupid ones!

I also remember the sadness I felt on November 5, 1952 as my platoon was learning to fire our M1 rifles. That was the morning we learned that Dwight D. Eisenhower had defeated Adlai Stevenson for President of the United States. How could America turn it's back on that erudite humanitarian Adlai Stevenson of Illinois with his Lincoln like sense of humor?

The worst night of bivouac was the first night when, at dark, I was pared with a stranger-soldier. Each of us took our "shelter halves" (we each had one half of a tent), to button them together to form a whole tent. It rained that night and the "tent" collapsed. At 33 degrees and with only my clothes and one blanket to keep me warm, I lay shivering for hours, my nose mere inches from the moisture-laden canvas, waiting for the morning bugle.

My thoughts went to Korea and the realization that if I felt frozen in the Virginia woods in November when the temperature was not below freezing, what would it be like in Korea in the winter when it would be 40 degrees below zero. I hate being cold, and at the moment I hated being in the Army.

II Basic Training to Okinawa

The end of basic training was the end of two months of mindless insanity. I never understood the army's idea that sleep deprivation would make you a good soldier. I came to understand that the prime purpose of basic training is to condition the soldier to follow orders strictly and blindly, without regard for common sense or safety. This might have worked had I been an unschooled 17-year-old country boy.

I don't remember that any part of basic training was physically difficult. The long marches, the calisthenics were handled with ease, and at the end of the eight weeks I knew I was stronger and I stood taller. At the end of my army career I was 160 pounds, and 6 feet 1½ inches in stocking feet, taller than before enlistment.

Toward the end of basic training an officer inquired if I would be interested in applying for OCS–Officers Candidate School. This was an offer I could easily and immediately refuse, as it would have been an additional two years in the service, and probable assignment to an infantry combat unit. The Korean War was in full force and Americans were dying by the hundreds. I had already come to regard the military as inefficient and ineffective and not an organization that was capable of meeting reasonable objectives without the squandering of human and material resources.

At the end of basic training each soldier was sent to C&A—Classification and Assignment. It was here that we were to be told what our army job would be and where we would receive the next eight weeks of training. Sitting behind the desk was a Second Lieutenant probably no longer out of college than I was. He studied my papers, and looked up cheerfully to tell me that "the Army" had decided I should become a Duck driver. Fort Eustis was a transportation base and a Duck was an amphibious truck used to ferry troops and supplies from ship to shore. They were heavily used during invasions and were vulnerable floating targets.

It wasn't so much the fear of being shot at that distressed me at this news, but the fact that after four years of college I thought I could be of much more value to the army than a "duck" driver. I told the second "loolie" that I didn't think that was an appropriate assignment and that if he didn't change it, I would complain to the Inspector General. At that, he replied that, "Okay, we'll send you to Transportation School, but, let me tell you if you flunk out, we'll do much worse than make you a Duck driver." And with that, I said thank you and left.

It was a pleasure to pack my gear and move from the basic barracks to a more settled part of Fort Eustis where we were housed in two-man rooms. Transportation School was designed to teach us about everything to do with moving goods and people. How to load airplanes and ships, how to prepare the manifests, and a hundred other things I can no longer recall. Unlike the first eight weeks, the class of privates consisted mainly of college graduates, with a few who held Masters degrees. School was pretty easy and we enjoyed our cigarette breaks and the opportunity to chat. Our evenings were free as were our weekends.

In the class was a contingent of Marines, mostly 18-year-old boys out of high school or almost out of high school. These young fellas are the ones who struggled to absorb the material. If it had not been for them, we could have probably finished the course in half the time.

I had become good friends with two Howards from New York City: Howard (Howie) Goodman and Howard Meizels. One day in the urinal, Howie, a Jew, quizzed me about my religious beliefs. Was I very religious? Did I believe in God? Did I believe Jesus was the Son of God? A week later, Howie invited me to come home with him to New York City. Everything about the weekend was a first: first visit to Gotham City (The Big Apple) and my first time on the subway. It was the last time I stayed in a swank apartment on Central Park West where the doormen showed us a respect we had never seen from any sergeant or lieutenant. On Saturday night we were taken to the fanciest of restaurants, where the women in our party, all svelte, well coifed, expertly made up and attractive, ate only a small portion of their food. They may have been mothers, but you would hardly notice. It was a memorable experience

The eight weeks of advanced basic training passed quickly and pleasantly at the end of which we had our "MOS"— Military Occupation Specialty"—which for us was "Military Transportation Control Specialist." It brought each of us our first stripe; we were now Privates, First Class (PFC). It also brought us a 30-day home leave and orders to report to Camp Stoneman, California, by the first of March 1953.

. . . . .

It was pleasant to be home in Columbus in my own bed and to be fed by my sweet mother. The time whizzed by and the most memorable moment of my home stay came in the last few minutes. Mamma fed me a last summer luncheon, and we talked. Then, lunch was done and it was time to call a cab for the trip to Port Columbus. When the cab came, I gave Mom a kiss and hug, shed a tear, said goodbye, picked up my duffle bag, and entered the cab.

It was a sad moment for Mom for she worried about her only son going off to war, perhaps never to return. I rolled down the cab window to say one last "goodbye" and the cab began moving slowly away, as if the driver knew that he should linger. Looking back, I saw Mama running after me for one last important instruction. She shouted through her tears, "And Abie," she cried, "don't bring home a Japanese girl."

. . . . .

California was a pleasant place to while away the hours. I don't know how I spent my 30 days at Camp Stoneman; the only specific duty I can recall is picking up cigarette butts and "field striping them," that is, tearing the cigarette paper apart so that the tobacco and ashes would fall to the ground. The paper was rolled into a small round speck and thrown to the ground where it became virtually invisible.

On the weekends I was free to leave the base and I did so without fail, going to my sister Alice's house on Friday night in Los Altos, south of San Francisco. She and her husband Jack welcomed me, fed me, entertained me, and let me do my washing, before sending me back to Camp Stoneman on Sunday evening. It was strange that during this month, I was a bifurcated individual. There was the army person and there was the civilian person, and when I was one, I could not remember being the other. The other self was so distant and foreign that surely, it must not exist. During the weekend, I could not remember what it was like to wear a khaki uniform or to eat army food or to smell army bodies. During the week, I had trouble remembering my sister's voice or those of her children or my brother-in-law's laughter.

My time at Camp Stoneman came to an end soon enough when I received orders for the "Far East." There were fourteen of us from advance transportation training and we all expected to be shipped out together, but strangely ten of the fourteen had orders to go to Japan, and the remaining four of us had orders to go to Okinawa. The destination of Japan was interpreted to be a way station to Korea, while Okinawa probably meant a less hostile assignment.

How did this happen? I was delighted with the assignment but puzzled. I asked Howie Goodman and Howard Meizels to explain it to me, but, no, they didn't know, they said. The two Howards had volunteered to work in the Stoneman personnel office because, as they said, they didn't want to be bored, and they didn't mind typing orders and other things. So Howard, Howard, Chris and Abe were off to Okinawa, wherever that was. But wherever it was, it wasn't Korea.

III Golden Gate to Armed Forces Radio

"**P**arting is such sweet sorrow," says Romeo to Juliet. And so it was as we boarded the Military Sea Transport Service ship near Martinez in Contra Costa County in late March 1953. The excitement of something new more than balanced the anxiety of the unknown. Many of the troops stayed topside to watch the 600-foot ship slip into San Francisco Bay, past the gleaming San Francisco skyline, and under the glorious Golden Gate Bridge.

The excitement ended quickly as the ship sliced through the typically turbulent waters that flow into and out of the bay. Suddenly, a nearby soldier's cigarette smoke became noxious, and caused my sense of balance and taste to fail me. I took out the pack of cigarettes from my shirt pocket and when the tobacco repulsed me, I threw the cigarettes into the ocean.

For the two-week duration of the oceanic cruise, I could not tolerate tobacco smoke, and I could stand without falling over only when I was topside and could orient myself against the horizon. In the bowels of the ship, I felt normal only when I was lying in my hammock.

Our dining mess was without chairs as we were required to eat standing up, a design intended to encourage the GI's to spend as little time at meals as possible, in order that all the soldiers could be served. I did my part by not eating in the mess. I lived for two weeks on oranges, crates of which were always available topside.

In order to prevent morale from sinking, most GI's were assigned some duty such as a kitchen helper, latrine cleaner, guard duty, etc. I was assigned to help with the daily newspaper, but my contribution was minimal, as I would use my *mal de mer* condition to excuse myself.

The canvas hammocks in the hold were my salvation; lying horizontal was vastly superior to a vertical position.

Fortunately, I had the second or third level of the tier of four hammocks. In the lowest hold where we were, the sea made the bottom hammock cold, and the steam pipes made the top hammock hot.

If my seasickness had not colored this experience in a negative way, I might have forgiven the MSTS, or the Army, for such low quality accommodations when compared to that accorded officers and their families who enjoyed waiter service and white tablecloths.

I am reminded now of my grandparents and parents who came across the north Atlantic in steerage, but without complaints. My grandfather arrived in New York on *The California*, a 300-foot, all steerage boat with a capacity of 1250 passengers. My mother was grateful she missed sailing on the Titanic by only ten months.

. . . . .

The first land spied in two weeks was Okinawa, a lush subtropic island with ground that did not sway and undulate. Our four-man transportation group was moved efficiently from boat to our new quarters, a well-painted, air-conditioned, stuccoed concrete block building with two-man rooms. The next day we reported to the Transportation Office and were greeted with a question: "What are you doing here? We didn't requisition you."

I was told to sit at a table and type some papers. After a short while, when I had earned a break from the heavy work, I made a visit to the nearby Armed Forces Radio Service station. I auditioned successfully as a radio announcer. The station's request to the Transportation unit was granted, and everybody was happy, especially me.

I moved my footlocker and duffle bag to the radio station's housing, a Quonset hut that was anchored to the ground with steel cables, a hopeful protection against each season's typhoons. The station was situated near Rycom Plaza atop a hill near Kadena Air Force Base. Our antenna served as a radio beacon to the B29 bombers on their way home from the bombing runs in Korea. There was no mistaking the bombers presence.

My roommate was Charles (Charlie) Stewart of Watertown, NY, who was well educated, intelligent, kind, and politically savvy. He was a well-informed Democrat. We have remained lifelong friends, writing to each other each year, talking on the telephone, and occasionally visiting. Through Charlie, I have kept apprised on other radio station personnel such as Don Gill, Dick Ridgeway, Bill Eaton, and others.

My job at the radio station was to be a DJ, and to write public service announcements. Unfortunately, we did not broadcast the news, relying on material shortwaved to us from AFRS headquarters for rebroadcast. As I had gone to college wanting to be a radio announcer, I was glad to have this opportunity to improve my announcing skills.

I once wrote a public service announcement on the general topic of conserving resources. The announcement began "Do you remember the Dutch boy who put his finger in the dike?" The spot was pulled the next day because all the island's troops were asking their friends if they were the one who had put their finger in the dyke. At any rate, it proved we had a large listening audience.

One highlight of our stay included a visit by Raymond Burr, the movie and television actor famous for his roles in Perry Mason and Ironside, who came to work with us to develop a radio drama. Our most exciting moments came with earthquakes and with the approach of a mighty typhoon. We speculated if our Quonset hut's cables would truly keep us anchored to the earth. We were doubtful.

I once got myself in trouble by angrily reacting to a rather stupid order by a new Second Lieutenant. He posted an order that said mistakes on the air would not be tolerated and we were to cease and desist from making any future goofs.

In anger my fist hit the wall where the announcement was posted, creating a hole in the soft wallboard. I argued that I had hit it with my elbow as I was exercising, a lame excuse indeed. The Lieutenant sent me to the Captain, sure that I would be disciplined, but the Captain though it a silly matter, and he accepted my suggestion that he give me a suspended suspension.

My work at the radio station was instrumental in helping me decide that I did not care for a career in broadcasting. Perhaps if we could have written and reported news I might have felt differently.

An announcement that there would be auditions for a new play resulted in a new direction for the remainder of my Army career.

IV "The Tea House of the August Moon"

In late 1953, The U.S. Army Ryukyuan Command on Okinawa had sought and received permission from the author and producer of the Broadway hit play *The Tea House of the August Moon* to produce the play on Okinawa with a combined military and civilian cast. It is very rare that an amateur production is allowed before closing on Broadway and before the end of its many national tours. But as the story was set on Okinawa, the producer, the well-known Maurice Evans and the author John Patrick, evidently felt that a limited run production 9000 miles from New York would not hurt them financially, and might even be good publicity. The proceeds of the production would go to the Ryukyuan American Friendship Committee for the purpose of building schools.

The Teahouse of the August Moon was a 1951 novel by Vern Sneider, and was adapted into a play by John Patrick, who later wrote the screenplay. As a play it won the Pulitzer Prize, the Tony Award and the Critics' Circle Award, and

was a great hit. It opened in October of 1953 and, after
1,027 performances, closed March 24, 1956. The original cast
included John Forsythe as Capt. Fisby, David Wayne as Sakini
and Paul Ford as Col. Purdy, all very well known stage and
screen actors. The director was the very well respected Robert
Lewis. A movie version opened in 1956 with Glenn Ford and
Marlon Brando.

When news of this upcoming production became known, I
applied, unsuccessfully, to be director of *The Tea House of the
August Moon*. This was not a great disappointment, as I had
had only limited directing experience during my college career.
I did, however, go to the acting auditions, winning the lead role
of Capt. Fisby, the role played by John Forsythe in the original
New York production.

The New York *World-Telegram* wrote that *Tea House
of the August Moon* "is one of the most successful plays of
the modern theater . . . A howling hit. It kept the premiere
audience rocking with ecstatic and uproarious laughter. This
is an enchanting play, filled with the most extraordinary good
sense about human and international relations." The *New York
Times* said the play was "completely captivating . . . delightful."

The play is a comedy about the process of the Americanization
of Japanese citizens on the island and the clash of cultures as a result.
Much of the comedy derives from the inability of American military
personnel to understand local culture and tradition.

A young military officer, Captain Fisby, is assigned to carry
out "Plan B" in a tiny Okinawan village, to begin the process of
Americanization by instituting a local democratic government,
establishing a capitalist economy, and building a schoolhouse in
which the village children will be taught English. Fisby is assigned
a local interpreter, Sakini, who attempts to explain to him many of
the local customs. Fisby, however, is frustrated when the villagers
are unable to market their local products, such as cricket cages and
lacquered bowls.

When Fisby appoints a local democratic government, they vote
to build a teahouse with the materials intended for the schoolhouse.
With the help of Lotus Blossom, a young geisha, Fisby quickly

becomes acclimated to the local culture and agrees to the building of the teahouse. In the meantime, he successfully markets a locally made brandy to the surrounding military bases.

When his commanding officer, Colonel Purdy, arrives, Fisby is caught in his bathrobe, a makeshift kimono, in the midst of a tea ceremony and is reprimanded for misusing military resources and for the selling of alcohol. Purdy orders the teahouse torn down and the distilleries destroyed—but the local villagers are clever and only pretend to carry out these orders while secretly preserving both. This proves fortunate, as Purdy learns that the village is to be presented as an example of successful democratization by Occupation Forces.

On the southern part of the island near Okinawa's capital city, Naha, there really is a *Tea House of the August Moon*, a Geisha house. Geishas are traditional, female Japanese entertainers, whose skills include performing various Japanese arts, such as classical music and dance. Contrary to popular opinion and stereotypes, geishas are not prostitutes and do not engage in sexual activity as part of their job.

The cast of 18 men, eight women, three children and one goat were filled with Americans and Okinawans, with only one of the Okinawan characters, Sakini, played by an American, Stephen Joyce. The main Okinawan female characters in the play is Lotus Blossom, a Geisha, played by 24-year-old Yukiko Hama, a real Geisha who was working at the real Tea House of the August Moon, a Geisha house.

The six-week rehearsal period went smoothly as the cast melded together seamlessly. Not all of the Okinawan actors could speak English, but many did. As a cast we grew together, and I for one, came to appreciate and love them. It was the most fortuitous event of my Army career, to be thrown into a group of people who

were alien to my culture and upbringing. Some of the Okinawan actors were professional actors but all of them met their responsibilities in a most professional way.

The director of the play was Glenn Pierce, who later took my place as a faculty member at Central Missouri State University. Stephen Joyce, who played Sakini, was an excellent actor who went on to a professional career in theatre. He won the 1983 Drama Desk Award as the Outstanding Feature Actor in a play for his role in the *Caine Mutiny Court-Martial*. Steve and I worked well together except for one incident.

Actors who share scenes—that is have equal dialogue—are taught to "share stage." This means that both actors are equally open to the audience. Joyce had a tendency on his lines to step up stage, away from the audience, forcing me to turn my back partially to the audience. This is called "upstaging" and is not considered friendly or ethical. As a counter, I would step up stage on my line so that we could again "share stage." As we had a dozen or more lines in this scene, we would end up standing far upstage, away from the audience. In time, I confronted Joyce about this and the practice stopped. But he was a good actor and was instrumental in making the play a success.

Glenn Pierce, Steven Joyce, and others of the American cast heavily courted Lotus Blossom. On our days off we sometimes spent hours in the Tea House restaurant enjoying hot tea and hot sake on the hot, humid days typical of Okinawa. I was also enamored of the very lovely Emmy (Amy) Omija who spoke excellent English. There were other Okinawans whose faces are embedded in my memory, if not their names. Photographs, however, make their presence real. Although I maintained no relationships with the American cast members, I remember some of their names: Robert Van Hook, Bob Wilson, Paul Savior, Steve Joyce, and Joe Ippilito.

The play was presented in a rather large auditorium, which seated about a thousand persons. We played each of the 30 performances to sold out houses, with audiences consisting mainly of American military and civilian persons but also a good number of Okinawans. When the show closed we had a very sad farewell party with tears flowing freely. A theatre production is an endeavor in which strangers come together for a common enterprise, which bonds them together. Ending that relationship is always sad and even painful.

At the end of the final performance, General D. A. D. Ogden, commanding general of the Ryukyuan Command, came on stage to thank all those who worked on the play, including the director and the cast. He proceeded to mention Sakini, Colonel Purdy, Lotus Blossom, and many other persons, but neglected to mention Capt. Fisby, my character. In spite of a stir in the audience, the General remained oblivious to his omission, for which I felt no pain. Things happen; it wasn't personal. The following week, I received a very nice letter from a Colonel Jackson, the commander of my unit, and later a second letter of commendation came from the commander of the Special Services unit. Finally, more than a month later, General Ogden wrote a personal letter of thanks.

The *New York Times* sent a reporter to write about our opening performance, which was published on April 23, 1954. I recall he asked me a question and that I was very disappointed with my response, whatever it was. The *Times* article was paired with another story of exactly the same length dealing with the opening of the play in London at Her Majesty's Theatre. The American actor Eli Wallach was Sakini. It was heady stuff indeed for me, a 23-year-old Army corporal to be mentioned in the *New York Times* and to have my picture in the June 14 issue of *Life Magazine*.

When I was cast in the production, I was transferred to the Rycom Rest Center, a resort facility on Okinawa's eastern beach. I had an air-conditioned room and a bed with clean sheets changed daily. We ate in a dining room with waiters serving us on tablecloth-covered dining tables.

· · · · ·

The House of Representatives passed a bill reducing the draft obligation to 12 months, and the US Senate to 24 months. The conference committee compromised at 21 months. When the play ended I was within two months of serving 21 months, and my application for an early discharge was granted. The orders were cut, my duffle bag packed and I and 187 other GIs were transported to the dock to load upon another 600-foot Military Sea Transport ship, which had arrived from Japan on the way to the United States.

Being loaded, our space aboard the ship was in the lowest hold. But the troops at the head of the line would not enter; they were reluctant to subject themselves to a two-week crossing in a dark, dank hold. I can hear the boarding sergeant begging the troops to board. It was the first time anyone in the army begged a soldier to do anything. He yelled, "Men, there are 188 bunks in your space, and there are 188 of you. Please go in and find your space."

The trip home was identical to the trip over: constant seasickness, hatred of cigarette smoke, inability to stand upright beneath the deck, inability to keep food down, and putrid johns. The only positive part of the trip was the knowledge that we were going home. So we enjoyed being topside, watching the phosphorescent lights created by the ship's propellers, playing cards top side and counting the hours to home.

The last night at sea saw most of the GIs on deck, straining to get a glimpse of lights along the Washington coast. Someone had a radio, and we thrilled to hear the sounds of music from a stateside radio station. Finally, in the early hours of the morning, we steamed into the Strait of Juan de Fuca, seeing the Port Angeles city street lights receding up toward the Olympic mountains, and finally into Puget Sound.

Our stay at Fort Lawton, in north Seattle, was relatively brief, and instead of taking the rails to Chicago, we were driven to Boeing Field in Seattle for a flight home. Packed into a four-motored propeller plane was endurable because now we were only hours from home. The plane took off and began circling in corkscrew fashion to gain altitude to pass over the Cascade Range and Mt. Rainier. An unscheduled stop was necessary in Omaha, Nebraska because the plane had run low on fuel. Some of us were able to exit the plane for a few moments, and it was a most remarkable moment. With the sun just rising over the hay fields that surrounded the airfield, I inhaled the fresh intense flavor of sweet clover. It was an unexpected revelation. I hadn't realized what I had missed. The memory of the clover let me endure the smell of stinking GI bodies on the last three-hour flight to Chicago.

Our discharge point was Fort Sheridan in Chicago. Standing in endless queues, waiting to be processed, we talked with soldiers who had been stationed around the world. Those of us from the Orient would always turn our heads to study and admire any Asian woman who walked by, while a soldier in front of me did the same with any black woman. He had been stationed in Kenya and had gone two years without seeing a white woman. It was a vivid reminder of how each of us had been changed during our service.

I don't know how I traveled home to Columbus, only that I had hitchhiked the last few miles. I had stripped my khaki's of all ornamentation, even my brass belt buckle, arriving home with only the clothes I wore. Although I had had good experiences in the service, I felt I had not made a worthy contribution. I went in the service vowing to be the best I could be, wanting to serve my country. I left feeling I did not achieve this goal. Arriving home with no mementos was a statement that since I was not really in the military the past 21 months, I should come home as if I had not been away. I made the most of my time in the Army and can only have wished that the Army had made the most of my time with them. I was now ready to resume my life.

MY ROARING TWENTIES
1950 - 1960

If the teens are the decade of uncertainty and insecurity, the twenties are about the gaining of confidence and self-esteem. So it was for me. I started my twenties as a college student and ended them as a college professor. I started the decade single and ended it married. In the beginning I was responsible only for myself but ended as a father. I began with carefree optimism and ended with weighty responsibility. As the decade proceeded each year ended better than the one before as I learned and matured.

Highlights of the decade were many: college graduation, service in the US army overseas in Okinawa, living and working in San Francisco, becoming a merchant seaman, studying and hitchhiking for nine months in Europe, enrolling in graduate school, gaining a master's degree, working at the university's radio and television station, meeting and marrying my wife and fathering a son.

Returning to the comfort of my mother's loving home following Army discharge found me feasting on the daily lettuce, tomato, and cucumber salads she made to fill my craving. My sisters Gladys and Selma were the co-managers at the Towne Tavern in downtown Columbus, and I strove to work with them. However, what the Long Street establishment needed more than another co-manager was expert management skills or a great infusion of cash. I had neither.

By the fall of 1954 I had made a decision to move to the San Francisco area where I could be near my West Coast family, Alice and Jack, Lorraine and Bill, and their children. The only impediment to traveling west was the application I had made

to become an FBI Special Agent. After all the pre-interview
conditions of completing forms were met, I took the train to the
Cincinnati office where the interview ended in thirty seconds.
"The FBI does not accept persons who wear glasses!"

I San Francisco to Paris

I arrived in California in late October and stayed with Alice
and Jack until early January, 1955 when I moved to the
Hilltop House at 1217 Jones Street atop Nob Hill. The co-ed
boarding house was catty-corner from Grace Cathedral, the
oldest Episcopal Church west of the Mississippi, and two
blocks from the St. Francis Hotel. There were 23 persons
living in the boarding house and we had 12 meals a week.
Aunt Louise, a jovial black woman, was the maid and cook,
and on Saturday's she would wake us by beating a ladle on a
pan, shouting "Hot Biscuits. Rise and Shine."

Making friends among so many young people was easy.
A great camaraderie was developed in short order. We did
things together: impromptu camping trips in the Sierra
Nevadas or at Big Sur or Mount Tamalpais; visits to the
Golden Gate or Seal Beach or the North Shore bars; or small
or large parties in the house. We also shared the affliction
of having little money as we worked in low-level career jobs.
But it made no difference because that year in the city was
the most carefree and exciting time in my life. I had also been
accepted into the San Francisco Drama Guild and Actors
Workshop, the first Equity Company outside of New York
City. I was cast in their production of John Millington Synge's
Deirdre of the Sorrows, a rarely performed play, and with
good reason.

I learned from my days in San Francisco that only one
friend really enjoyed working in the corporate world. People
came to San Francisco and stayed for a while before moving

on to Denver, Boston, Seattle or Chicago. I might have stayed longer had I been able to find a challenging position. I interviewed with virtually all the major corporations in the city and many minor ones. Although the corporation presidents were clamoring for liberally educated young people, they neglected to tell their personnel directors to look out for these smart young persons. During the year my thoughts returned to the possibility of being a college teacher.

By the early winter of 1955, I had decided I would enter graduate school, but first I would go to Paris to learn French, a requirement for graduate school. One-by-one the barriers fell: approval for the GI bill; admittance to the *Cours de Civilisation Française de la Sorbonne*; certification as a Merchant Seaman (to work my way to or from overseas); free transportation from California to New York; passage overseas; housing at the University of Paris.

Arriving in New York in February 1956, I immediately bought passage on a Cunard ship bound for Le Harve. Within a week or so I was in Paris. I purchased room and board for three weeks and was broke. It is frightening to be in a foreign country unable to speak the language and to have no money. But then thoughts of my mother arriving in New York at 21 years of age with no knowledge of English and no money in her pocket gave me the greatest admiration for her spunk. It would be six weeks before my first GI bill check would arrive, if it was on time. Unable to borrow money from any source, I turned to my sister Alice and her husband Jack, and they obliged with a check for $100. When I returned to the states, that money was paid back $10 monthly until the debt was gone.

The French course was already in its second semester, so catching up was out of the question. I studied as best as I could and by the end of the term found I could order tickets, ask for directions, read simple signs. In hindsight, I regret I could not have spent the entire year in Paris. Our teacher was

Mlle. Cahier (sic), a svelte and winsome lass in her twenties with long straight hair who I remember most for her delicious body odor. (It may have been perfume, but I am not sure.) Her image came back most strongly to mind fifty years later when at the Henrik Ibsen Museum in Oslo, Norway, a young guide had the same body odor.

Concert going in Paris was a *de rigeur* activity. The French concert venues allowed those with a valid student identification to buy last minute tickets at a very low price. The seats were often in the best sections, and one might find themselves seated next to a woman in a georgeous gown or a man in a tuxedo. I attended three or four concerts a week. At one concert I was introduced to Schubert's Death and the Maiden (*La Jeune Fille et La Morte*) performed by the then young Amadeus Quartet. It was the beginning of a life-long love affair with chamber music. At concerts I kept running into Addie Vroegop, a Dutch girl, and we established a friendship that lasted many years.

After the term at the Sorbonne ended I arranged for my trunk to be sent home and purchased a French rucksack (backpack), loading it with a sleeping bag and extra pair of shoes and the other minimal items required for months of hitchhiking in Europe.

II Hitchhiking Through Europe

Here are highlights of that glorious experience.

Hitchhiking from **Paris to Geneva** I was accompanied by a young American female student who I had hoped would entice more drivers to offer rides. This was a failed notion. When we finally reached Switzerland, a few miles from our destination, night had fallen, the temperature was dropping, and traffic had come to a standstill. Our options were two: continue standing in the dark and in the cold and wait for a car, or get in the sleeping bag and be warm but uncomfortable until dawn. The dilemma was solved when a car finally appeared, stopped, and drove us to Geneva. My destination was to the apartment of friends of a friend, but as it was midnight, and the apartment lights were out, I decided to unfurl my sleeping bag under an upturned rowboat on the shore of Lake Geneva. It was the next morning when the friends of my friend welcomed me. (Young people can be so gracious and welcoming.)

Mont Blanc presented me with the most agonizing decision on my trip. Always interested in high mountains, I wished to ride the téléférique at Chamonix, France, to the high meadows of Mt. Blanc. But the cost was 6 dollars, twice my daily budget. I spent an hour trying to make the budget work in my favor. But it wouldn't and with great sadness, I passed up this adventure.

With **Aix en Provence** my destination, I again ran out of daylight and traffic. The only solution was to unfurl the sleeping bag and find a spot in the field that was as comfortable as possible. This is the night that I learned about the *mistral*, that strong, cold, constant wind that comes pouring down from the northwest to the Mediterranean Sea. It is difficut to sleep with the sound of tree branches cracking and popping throughout the night. I was up at day break, and it was my fortune that the first car on the road stopped to bring me to my destination.

A young Italian couple in **Genova** invited me for dinner. A year later, I received an invitation to their wedding but could not afford to send a wedding present, which I rue even today.

Traveling about with a rucksack on your back and staying in youth hostels meant meeting many young people from around the world. One connection would always lead to another. Travel tips were traded: how to obtain a free meal ticket in Italy, how to get concert and museum tickets at reduced rates, where to stay in your next city. In Genoa, the consensus was that one should not hitchhike to Rome; the train was the much better option.

In **Rome**, I spent a full day in the Roman Forum, and I ate for free in a soup kitchen. The minestrone was good and filling. In the hostel in Rome one person had a car. A group of four of us traveled to Innsbruck, sharing gasoline expenses. In the Italian Dolomites the car broke down. Serendipitously, there was a garage within yards. The repair took only a short while and the cost was very low.

The food in **Innsbruck** was very cheap and I treated myself to a delicious small pastry. But the many other times I stopped by a bakery in European countries, I only looked at the baked goods through the window, devouring with my eyes, before walking on.

Wiesbaden near **Frankfurt-am-Main, Germany**, is where my first cousin Air Force Col. John Isper Saad was stationed. I had never met his wife Mary, so when the door opened, and an attractive woman greeted me with a southern accent, I said, "Hello, Mary!" But it wasn't Mary but the German maid who had worked for many years with US military families, most of whom had southern accents.

Hitchhiking in Germany taught me not to be too facile with a foreign language. I had a decent ear for languages and could memorize phrases and pronounce them well. In Germany I was taught to say: "Ich bin nach München!" In France, I would say "Je vais à Genève." But my decent prononciation only invited a response in a language that I had not mastered. I learned to speak very slowly, very clearly, and with simple sentences. And I always learned to say "please" and "thank you" in the native language.

In **Copenhagen, Denmark**, I arrived late at night,

despairing of finding a hostel. I decided to board the first tram that came by, riding it to the end of the line. There were no street lights but I found a clump of bushes that allowed me to lay out my sleeping bag and fall asleep. I awoke the next morning to the animated chatter of a group of women. The bushes were in an area surrounded by apartments. I took the same tram back to city center to find a hostel.

Later that day, I was standing by a downtown corner when a local Dane approached me to begin a conversation. Before leaving he asked if he and his wife and small daughter could meet me the next night and show me their city. "Yes, of course; thank you." And so they did. I spent several hours with them seeing the sights of this delightful city and afterwards spent time in their apartment.

Eindhoven, the **Netherlands,** was a destination because I had been invited to visit Addie Vroegop, the friend I met in Paris. Her family was very gracious, and they arranged for me to visit the Phillips factory where I saw the manufacture of light bulbs. I learned that the Dutch had great respect for Americans because our Army's 101st Division had liberated their country in World War II. Addie and I exchanged Christmas cards for many years, until one year she asked where we had met. It was time to let go.

Sonderberg, Denmark, just north of Schleswig-Holstein, Germany, was a destination because of an invitation from Annalisa Nielsen, a good friend I had met in San Francisco. Uncle Willie and his family introduced me to Akvavit, the Dane's national drink made from grain or potatoes, basically Scandinavian Schnapps. They were very gracious hosts.

Arriving in **England**. Coming through passport control at Dover, the official stamped my passport as valid for only 30 days as I did not have sufficient financial resources to stay longer. One of the joys of coming to England is that one is relieved of having to deal with a foreign language. The first time I spoke to an Englishman after arriving in Dover was for the purpose of getting the time of day. The reply was that he did not speak English.

In **London**, exiting the tube at Earls Court, I heard a voice shout, "Abe, Abe!" It was a girl I had met in Rome. "What are you doing here?" I replied that I came to this area of London to find a room where I could stay a week. She told me that her house was nearby and space was available. So that was my spot for the week. I couldn't get over the low price of theatre tickets in London. I saw *Plain and Fancy*, at Drury Lane Theatre for 65 cents.

Hitchhiking in England was generally good, but no one could beat Peter Ross, a Scot who wore kilts. Drivers skidded their tires stopping to pick him up.

A destination in England was the Yorkshire district near the North York Moors National Park. Near the town of Thrisk was a small village, Sutton-under-Whitestonecliffe, where I was invited to visit by Rosemary Chaflin, whom I had met in Paris. I can still picture her father; he with a woolen sports coat worn over a sweater and shirt with tie, even as he went outside to tend the cattle. He was a prototypical country Englishman.

I left England before my thirty days had expired, traveling to Ireland where I stayed for three weeks before returning to Liverpool, England. Had passport control asked to know my wealth they might have denied me entry. I found an inexpensive room where if you wanted hot water for bathing you had to drop a penny into the meter that controlled the flow of gas to the hot water heater. Showers were short. Each day in Liverpool I traveled to docks to find a ship on which I might work my way home. Down to my last ten dollars, and ready to return to London to find a job, I was hired as an able-bodied seaman on the SS Charles Lykes, bound for New Orleans.

The reader can see why I described my months in

Europe as an extremely heightened and vital life experience. Everywhere I went I found gracious and kind people who befriended me and taught me about their country and their way of living. Whenever a young person has said they would like to travel or live overseas, I have been most supportive and encouraging.

III My Wife Sharon

In the fall of 1958, I met Sharon when we were cast in a two-person play at Ohio State. Each of us, seeking a break from our daily routines, found our wish in Tennessee Williams's *Mooney's Kid Don't Cry*, directed by a graduate student and produced in the Derby Hall Theatre. In this short one-act play I am Mooney, a frustrated laborer having an argument with an ailing wife. When she slaps my face, I catch her by the throat and toss her to the floor. She tells me to leave, but insists I take the baby with me, placing it in my arms. It was a complication that befuddled Mooney.

The play was a fun experience, which we both enjoyed with one exception. The wife slaps Mooney's face, which done

correctly is painless. However, Sharon's aim was off, and it was my ear and not my cheek that absorbed the blow. My subsequent throwing her to the ground was probably a little stronger than the script called for, but our director loved the realistic acting.

After one of our rehearsals I offered to ride Sharon back to her dormitory on my bicycle. On that particular night, an overweight girl friend had accompanied Sharon. I put both of them on my bike and proceeded to cross the oval and ride by Mirror Lake. We hit a dip in the path and I had to walk the rest of the way to the dorm because the weight of my passengers had bent the frame of the bicycle.

Handing Mooney the play's baby was a prophetic moment; we did argue, we did marry, we did have a baby, and we did have some frustrating times, but we avoided the violence. We met in the fall of 1958 and we were married in June of 1959. I had taken my written comprehensive examinations in the spring of 1959, and nothing can be more frightening. I remember one afternoon—it was a three-day ordeal—Sharon came into the office where I was contemplating one of the essay questions. It was a welcome but momentary relief from the fear that I hadn't the slightest idea how I was going to offer an essay in response to the esoteric and baffling questions posed by one of the professors. Sharon looked at me, sensing my ensuing panic, and reassured me that I would do fine.

I passed the orals and shortly after that successfully  auditioned for an announcing position at the University radio stations, WOSU-AM and FM. The way to marriage was now clear with my incredible salary of $3675 per annum. Sharon had just completed her junior year in college. After our marriage we moved into my apartment in the attic of my mother's duplex near the University, and I assumed responsibility for paying Sharon's tuition for her senior year. Sharon graduated on June 12, and on the 20th of June 1960, our son Douglas was born on the anniversary of our wedding date. (Years later when Douglas married, he chose to do so on June 20th, his birthday, our anniversary, and in that year on Father's Day).

In the summer of 1960 I was urged by my advisors to

accept the position of Instructor at Central Missouri State College, even though the position teaching broadcasting and television is not one I had trained for. It was my practical experience in broadcasting that led to the job. Sharon and I moved to Warrensburg and found a second-floor apartment overlooking the campus, and we settled in to learn new roles as teacher and father, and faculty wife and mother.

Sharon was extremely pretty and made the best strawberry pies imaginable, a skill that always made us welcomed at faculty gatherings. As it was very intimidating for Sharon to be a young person less than three months out of college to be affiliating with (sometimes stuffy, older) Ph.Ds and Ed.Ds and their wives, we did a lot of hand-holding. But we got to know younger faculty, quickly discovering that most of them were recent graduates and had only a few years teaching experience. Overall, they were very good teachers, and our students had the opportunity to gain a great education. As cash was not in great supply, we met for potluck dinners at various homes. It was fun and a great learning experience for both of us.

My pay came in ten installments, so Sharon and I had to carefully budget our resources in order to return to Columbus the next two summers so that I could work on my dissertation. Sharon could not have been more helpful. She allowed me to go off to work each morning at 8 o'clock, returning at 5 in the evening. She did the shopping, housework, tended to our son, without ever imposing a list of honey-do's. Completing the dissertation was a very important thing for both of us.

In the first ten years of our married life, we moved about the country following the job market, each time improving our salary and living conditions. Our mothers and family came to visit us in Missouri, Washington and North Dakota, and we on occasion traveled home. We discovered that on returning to Ohio after those years, we were accepted by the family as a mature and independent couple. We were as glad to be among family as they were pleased to have us.

Our ten years, however, had some frightfully difficult periods, particularly for Sharon. In Warrensburg, Missouri, Sharon suffered a grievous injury in the supermarket when an errant bottle of soda pop fell to the floor, exploding and sending shards of glass, one such cutting the tendon in her left foot. In spite of her protests, the doctors assured her it was a minor cut of minor significance. When we finally saw a foot and ankle specialist he opined that with surgery there might be at best a 50/50 chance of helping. We declined the opportunity.

At age 24, in August 1963, Sharon miscarried, and less than two months later she suffered a tubal pregnancy. Thinking she was again miscarrying, the doctor sent her home for two weeks with a ruptured fallopian tube. The physical and emotional damage was daunting.

Pregnancy came again in Washington State at age 25, and it was a very successful pregnancy until the last week. "I can't feel the baby move," she cried to me. Our baby girl was stillborn. The umbilical cord had wrapped around the baby's neck, and our little girl suffocated. She was normal in every way and only two days from delivery. We were devastated. One cannot lose a child without frequently wondering what she would have been, who she would have favored, what would be her dominant characteristics.

Six months later we received a call from our pediatrician Dr. Bass, asking if we would be interested in adopting an infant boy. Yes, of course, and we had the child before we were vetted by the county welfare agency. We named him Andrew Jordan Bassett. He was eight months old before the child welfare people returned him to their custody. He was physically and mentally damaged and not suited for adoption.

Five months later, as we healed, the same Dr. Bass called to say that he had a healthy, normal baby for adoption. "Would we be interested?" Our answer was immediate. "Yes, of course. When can we pick her up?" Two days later we went to the Tacoma General Hospital to bring home a petite, pretty baby girl, whom we named Valerie. So now we had a girl to go with our boy.

V | THE ACADEMY

MY FIRST REAL JOB
1960-1963

The first job is the hardest to get, and the first job is the hardest to do.

Why would any college want to hire a person just out of graduate school with no teaching experience? Knowing the difficulty of finding that first job, my advisors at Ohio State recommended that I accept the position at Central Missouri State College with the rank of Instructor, even though it was a position I was not excited about and not qualified for by training or education. In those days, the interviewing institution paid your travel expenses only if they offered the job and you accepted the position. Otherwise, the expenses came out of the interviewee's pocket, which, in this case, required that I drive the 650 miles to Warrensburg, Missouri from Columbus. When I arrived, rather tired, at what I thought was the main junction of the town, I drove through it finding myself in country. I had to turn around to take a spur road to the main part of the town.

The interview was a success, and with no other prospects in hand I accepted the position. I had, I thought, been offered the position of Assistant Professor at an annual salary of $5,900, but when the contract arrived it was for $5,500 and the rank of Instructor. The position in the Department of Speech had been advertised at the higher rank, but for a person with the Ph.D. in hand. I was "ABD" or "All But Degree" as it was popularly known. Still, $5,500 was an increase of $1,800 for a nine-month contract, compared to the $3,700 earned in 12 months at the Ohio State University as an announcer-writer for WOSU-AM-FM-TV. A trend was set; as I took new positions over the years, it always came with a substantial salary increase.

How was it that I was hired and so late in the year in June 1960? Bill Dodge, the Department Chair, said they were attracted by my practical experience in radio. They wished to install a campus radio station and that became my prime extracurricular assignment. But, cynically perhaps, to answer the real question why would a person of no experience be hired, the real reason is that this person was cheap and could easily be overworked and abused. With some luck the institution might actually have hired a good worker, who met his assignments and didn't complain. That description applies to me.

As an instructor in the Department of Speech I was to teach three classes each quarter in addition to the radio station assignment, which consumed more hours than any course. Those courses included Public Speaking, Mass Communication, History of Broadcasting, Phonetics, Acting, and three other courses. All in all, I taught nine courses in that first year, with only one of the classes repeated. That is eight new course preparations. Anyone who has taught a new course knows how much work goes into preparation. Everyone knows that eight preparations in nine months is a truly prodigious if not laughable feat.

My very first class was a mass lecture in Public Speaking at 8:00 a.m. on the first day of the quarter. I had been up until 3:00 a.m. making notes from textbooks. That first lecture lasted 40 minutes and at the end I turned to Dr. Paul Reid, the coordinator of Public Speaking, to know–of all things–if I had made any grammatical errors in my presentation!

Sharon and I lived in an upstairs apartment over the landlord, Mrs. Marty. The house was adjacent to the campus, only minutes from my office. My office was literally a janitor's closet with no windows or air conditioning. Mrs. Marty was an old-fashioned lady who chided my language when I once said that I was "pooped." We were comfortable in that upstairs furnished apartment which had a balcony that faced the campus, but we didn't spend much time socializing with Mrs. Marty.

When the first Friday afternoon came and my week's work done, I came home in total exhaustion. I hadn't had more than five hours sleep each night, never more than a 30-minute lunch, and a 45-minute dinner. My nights were spent preparing the next day's lectures. Fortunately, I read the textbook assignments better than my students. I noted that some faculty had leisurely lunches and collegial discussions with the topic often nothing more serious than last night's television fare. We did not own a television set. Sharon read novels, and I read textbooks. It was a miracle that I survived week one, but I had no faith that I could keep up this pace for ten weeks, followed by ten weeks in the winter and ten weeks in the spring. The prospect of thirty weeks of little sleep and high tension was glum indeed.

I was never a person who worshiped money, who needed material things to ensure happiness, but with a wife and a baby son to support, there was no thought of quitting. I learned to take each day, class by class, assignment by assignment, thinking only of completing the next item on the agenda.

There were some respites from the tension that year. The basketball team was quite good and I attended the Saturday evening games. The coach was Gene Bartow, who rose in the coaching ranks, eventually to coach at UCLA replacing the legendary John Wooden. There were potluck faculty gatherings that Sharon and I attended. Because of Sharon's excellent strawberry pies, we were especially welcomed. And because the college's faculty was very young with recent Ph.Ds. and ABDs, we developed friendships with other faculty, many of them with young families with little extra cash to spend, making potluck suppers a Saturday evening entertainment norm.

Our six-man Department faculty meetings were always

exciting. As the new man, I had very little to say as I listened and learned. There were a series of contentious arguments between Drs. Paul Reid and Shef Pierce. My head swung from side to side as if I were at a tennis match trying to follow their arcane and academic (and probably personal) arguments.

The day before spring quarter classes began, Bill Dodge, the department chairman, asked if I would teach a class in Phonetics. "But Bill," I protested, "I have had only one class in phonetics and that was as an undergraduate eleven years ago, and I was a "B" student." Bill insisted, saying I could do it, and that Dr. Lin Welch, our speech pathologist who normally taught the class, would assist me. Well, Lin did assist me: he let me use his Phonetics textbook.

Again, I read each chapter one day ahead of the students, and I came to class reasonably prepared. Halfway through the quarter, a mature black student who was in another of my classes said to me that the students had figured out that I concentrated mainly on one of the three classes I taught each quarter. When he had asked a question about a topic we had not covered, my answer was, "hold on, we are coming to that next week."

The beauty about teaching is that it is a great learning experience for the teacher. I came to enjoy the Phonetics class a great deal, and I used what I had learned for the remainder of my teaching and directing career. One of the things I loved to teach was the development and proper use of the actor's voice. Voice and Diction, we called it then. Phonetics was central to that study.

When my sister Alice came east from California to visit family she stopped for a short while in Warrensburg. I tried to dissuade her from observing my teaching, but she managed to find the classroom and stood in the hallway out of sight but not out of listening range. I think she was disappointed that the phonetics class was not more philosophical.

My prime extra curricular assignment that year was to develop a campus radio station. We were assigned a space in the main administration building underneath what would have been the "observatory," had a telescope ever been purchased. Somehow I found a student who knew about radio circuits, and with my prodding he built, from scratch, what was known as a Carrier Current transmitter. By attaching the signal to the college's electrical grid, our signal could be heard throughout the campus. We found funds to buy some microphones and we dressed up the announcing booths. I wrote to record companies to get on their list for distribution of recordings to campus radio stations.

One of my best students who was interested in radio broadcasting was Gary Nunn, who later went on to a career in broadcasting with ABC radio in New York. Gary was a very mature and a well-disciplined young person with a fine radio voice. In my second year, together we developed a weekly fifteen-minute broadcast of editorials from Missouri newspapers. Each week, a tape of the program was sent to radio stations throughout Missouri, gaining notoriety for our campus. The program was carried on Warrensburg's one commercial station, the owner of which also owned the local newspaper. He was enamored of the program and wrote an editorial complimentary to me. The editorial was titled "The Man With The Golden Voice."

The reach of the campus radio station was sporadic and weak so in my second year we investigated the possibility of purchasing a ten-watt transmitter. When the newspaper owner heard of the plan, he strongly objected, fearing competition. When I reported this conversation to our feisty President, Warren Lovinger, he immediately authorized the expenditure for the transmitter. We were soon on the air with programming typical of University-based public radio stations, our model being those at Ohio State University where I had worked while in graduate school. We developed several faculty-moderated programs, played classical music, and presented news programs by training students to rewrite stories from the New York Times and other newspapers. This was the beginning of KCMW-FM, [**K** Central **M**issouri **W**arrensburg] which is now a 50,000-watt NPR station whose signal is heard in Kansas City. Call letters were changed some years ago and the station is now KTBG. Central Missouri State College became Central Missouri State University, and recently changed its name to the University of Central Missouri, which is curious because it is the University of Missouri that is near the state's center.

Surviving that first year of teaching was either a mystery or a miracle. It was the hardest thing I have ever done. But there were highlights. I did get a chance to teach a class in beginning Acting two times, the only repeated course of the year. In the spring of the following year, I was given the opportunity to direct a play and I chose *The Rainmaker*. I remember my student actors well and wish I could visit with each of them: Marganne Geis, Ron Lavor, Rich Low, and Bernie Lawson. The play was presented in the round in the Pit Theatre and was well attended and well received. The actors played their parts with great earnestness and theatrical truth. Jim Highlander, the titular head of the theatre section, remarked (perhaps condescendingly) that the play was much better than he thought it would be.

We spent three years in Warrensburg learning a great deal about the art of teaching and developing many friendships throughout the college. So many young faculty who had their first jobs here moved on to other institutions, and we were able to say that after three years we had friends all around the United States.

Sharon and I made a brief visit to Warrensburg several years ago and discovered that although the University had name changes, the town had changed very little. It was the same seedy, unkempt, and uncared for town. The pride of the city is the bronze statue of a dog, "Old Drum," immortalized by George Vest in 1870 as "man's best friend." In the spring, during the time we lived in Warrensburg, students would spray red paint on the dog's genitals. The following morning city workers would conceal the dirty deed in brown wrapping paper, and there would follow an editorial decrying the moral decay of the younger generation and the lack of respect for Old Drum. This is why we often referred to our city as Warrensdog.

TEACHING IN THE PACIFIC NORTHWEST
1964-1968

I was hired at Pacific Lutheran University in Tacoma, Washington without getting any closer to the campus than Chicago, Illinois! The key to that fact is that this was a "Lutheran" institution and its directors and leaders were Norwegians known for frugality. This characteristic has paid off, for today Norway is the richest country in the world and is totally without debt.

I interviewed on the telephone with the Chairman of the Department of Speech, Dr. Ted Karl, but it was the President, Dr. Robert Mordvedt, who interviewed me in the lobby of the Palmer House Hotel in downtown Chicago. As I had once applied to and been accepted by the graduate school at the University of Washington in Seattle, I had a very positive attitude about moving from Missouri to the great Pacific Northwest.

When the contract came, I was horrified, running to my dictionary to learn the meaning of "evangelical" and how the word is pronounced. "I can't sign this contract," I screamed to Sharon. "I am not an 'evangelical' person." Sharon adamantly screamed back, "SIGN IT!" And so I did, but only after I covered the offending sentences with my hand.

This occurred in the summer of 1964 when I was directing plays at Ohio University's summer theatre in Athens. By August first, we were ready to leave Ohio and camp our way to Parkland, a suburb of Tacoma, the home of Pacific Lutheran. There was no need to rush to Washington as our goods were being shipped and the moving company said our goods would arrive in about 30 days!

We had purchased a homemade camping trailer brilliantly designed by an Economics professor using surplus army bunks for their angle iron steel frames. The camper, built to sleep four, was erected atop a 4' by 6' trailer. Canvas was sewn to provide divided storage under the bottom bed. It worked very well and provided us with cheap lodging as we discovered and enjoyed attractions along the way: the Corn Palace, The Badlands, Wind Cave, Mt. Rushmore, Yellowstone National Park, and finally the Cascade Mountains. When we arrived in Western Washington we camped in a state park as we searched for a place to live.

We soon found a lovely, affordable three-bedroom house on 120th street in Parkland, which allowed me to walk to work and even walk home for lunch. But the better thing was that we had lovely, lovely neighbors: ordinary folks who were warm, kind, open, welcoming, and unpretentious. We quickly got to know them well enough to be able to walk in for a cup of coffee or tea. One neighbor offered to baby-sit Douglas so Sharon and I could spend a weekend together. Another neighbor extended offers to troll for lake trout, an activity so lovely, I had no disappointment when my catch was nil. We once went fishing in the Pacific Ocean for salmon. I built a kitchen storage cabinet for one neighbor. The house across the street had two girls who were great playmates for Douglas. We lived here for four years, renting for two years before we bought.

The faculty at the University was also warm but not as quick in accepting a new couple until two years had passed. Now, 45 years later, we still communicate with faculty, neighbors, and some students.

If I had trepidation about working in a religiously oriented university, they were reinforced at the faculty meeting that took place before classes started. Dr. Olaf Jordahl, professor of Physics, had the severe demeanor of a pastor in an Ingmar Bergman movie. Actually, however, as I got to know him, he was a lovely, gentle person whose inside was nothing like his outside.

A second frightening presentation at that first faculty meeting was religious professor Kenneth Christopherson who rose to make a presentation. His powerful voice was modulated like a police siren: loud and then soft, up and then down, seemingly without regard to meaning. But, like the Physics professor, he was a nice person. Being a show-off doesn't qualify one as a scary person.

I once accepted his invitation to hike to Camp Muir high on the side of Mt. Rainer. Solid stone cabins at exactly 10,000 feet serve as a final stage for ascending the summit of Mt. Rainer. The hikers sleep a little bit before departing at three a.m.; the early start allows for a return the next afternoon. To reach Camp Muir one must traverse the Muir snowfield, which is actually a glacier, but an extremely slow moving one. Living at nearly sea level and climbing to 10,000 feet is very difficult. The routine is established: one step, a second step, stop, breathe, repeat. As one climbs higher, climbing into cleaner air, the clear blue sky becomes a darker blue. The vista soon includes other volcanic peaks along the Cascade's Ring of Fire, including Mt. St. Helens, Mt. Adams and Mt. Hood.

Professor Christopherson once led some students to summit Mt. Rainer. Bad weather forced them to turn back, but one student, separated from the others, took a wrong turn ending on a precipice at Gibraltar Rock, unable to descend further and too weak to retrace his steps for lack of oxygen. The Professor stayed with the student until the day following they were rescued by a helicopter that made the highest flight ever on Mt. Rainier. The student was one of mine.

Teaching was a pleasure because we had good students. It was a particular pleasure to direct musicals because Lutherans go to church regularly and they learn to sing at an early age. When President Mortvedt told us we had to produce *The Song of Norway* one year, we cast the lead soprano because she was a senior. Any of a dozen girls could have been cast. When I directed *Carousel*, I doubt if any undergraduate school in the United States could have had three better voices for the three male leads. They were superb singers and good actors, thanks to their Lutheran upbringing. Our music department's choirs were good, but St. Olaf University in Minnesota, another Lutheran college, had the reputation of having the best choir in the country.

When I directed Shakespeare's *Romeo and Juliet* I spent many hours trying to find a fight choreographer, with no success. The day fall semester classes began, a freshman girl knocked on my door. "Dr. Bassett," she said, "I understand you need a fight choreographer for Romeo and Juliet." She gave me her credentials and I engaged her on the spot. At our first fight rehearsal, she came in the white uniform that fencers wear, causing our male actors to snicker. In about 10 minutes, when the actors were sweating, and the instructor's expertise established, the snickering stopped.

Romeo and Juliet was my first attempt at directing Shakespeare and needing time to prepare, I took the camper to Mt. Rainier for three days of uninterrupted work. I achieved my goal of preparing the script, but I learned how lonesome I could become without my family.

My favorite class turned out to be "Oral Interpretation I," which I taught every semester, getting better and better each term. The class was always filled to capacity, and my students learned a great deal about using their voices to convey the emotion and feelings of the literature they selected. But I also learned a great deal as they introduced me to literature I did not know.

In the summers of 1966 and 1967, our campus became the summer home of the Joffrey Ballet. They concluded their stay by performing the ballets they had constructed and rehearsed.

I was able to see all of their performances, becoming enamored of their form of dance, with their emphasis on dramatic story telling. Years later while at Wright State University, I was invited to serve on the board of the Dayton Ballet, where the Artistic Director, Stuart Sebastian, choreographed story-telling works. These experiences were important in guiding me in the development of our dance program at Wright State.

We loved our time at Pacific Lutheran and in the great Pacific Northwest, leaving there with the thought that this would be the place of our retirement.

OUTDOORS IN THE PACIFIC NORTHWEST
1964-1968

If you drove the streets of Parkland, Washington, where we lived for four years, or any other town in the Pacific Northwest, you would discover that every third house had a boat or a camper.

We quickly learned to enjoy the great outdoors in the Cascade Mountains or Olympic Peninsula, as well as the many other natural attractions of the region.

In our 48 months in the state I visited Mt. Rainier National Park at least once a month. It was a two-hour drive to Paradise, 5400 feet above sea level, the site of a Visitor Center and a Lodge, and the starting place for treks to the summit of 14,410-foot Mt. Rainier. We visited as a family, or sometimes, Douglas and myself, and sometimes myself alone on a Saturday or a holiday. We visited in the winter and summer, often hiking above Sunrise to get better views of the glaciers. At a certain elevation one could spot Mt. Adams, Mt. St. Helens, and on a clear day, Mt. Hood in Oregon.

I had one trek to Camp Muir situated exactly at 10,000 feet. Here was a stone lodge where those who climbed to the summit slept, arising at 3 a.m. to begin their ascent. They first walked or crawled, roped together, across a small bridge on the glacier, best done in the dark, because on either side of the bridge is a long drop into the bowels of the glacier.

At the Visitor's center a Park Ranger told of the story of a horse, laden with supplies to replenish the stores at Camp Muir, that fell into a crevasse on the Muir snowfield. Understanding that it would be impossible to rescue the horse, the rangers descended to the park headquarters to get a gun to put the horse out of its misery. When they returned they discovered the horse had disappeared. His body heat had melted the ice and he had disappeared into the depths of the glacier, not to be seen or found ever again.

Every year one or two or more people died on Mt Rainier, having been caught in a storm or avalanche. Some people were able to save their lives by seeking shelter in a shallow crevasse, avoiding the killing winds.

Once at Paradise when we slept out, not in a tent, but in our sleeping bags, we arose in the moonless night to discover no need for a flashlight. One could read by starlight. ("Starlight, star bright...")

Douglas and I also packed in the Olympic National Park where we spent an overnight. I loaded Douglas' backpack with bulky, items but not heavy items, such as pots and pans. Coming across a troop of boy scouts, the scoutmaster made his troop study Douglas' seemingly oversized load. "Look at the boy." He shouted. "Look at that load. Do you see him complaining? I don't want to hear any more complaints." Douglas stood proud, I was amused, and we trudged on to our camping site.

BIG SKY COUNTRY
1968-1970

We moved to North Dakota in the summer of 1968 when I accepted a position as Professor and Chair of the Department of Speech Theatre at Dickinson State College, now a University. Dickinson is located in the west central part of the state, about 80 miles east of the Montana border, giving itself permission to refer to itself as part of The Big Sky Country. The city was also close to the Theodore Roosevelt National Monument (now a National Park), and the North Dakota Badlands. One could not live in this part of the west without being aware of the natural majesty of the land and in awe of the weather,

North Dakota weather, summer or winter, was unpredictable, dangerous, but always exciting. Of all my memories of our two years in that northern plains state, it is the weather that is most vivid. But I do remember a number of my excellent students and the plays we produced, especially the two seasons of the outdoor Sosondowah Summer Theatre. The relationships that result from working together on a play are often intense, meaningful and long lasting.

I first came to Dickinson without Sharon to interview for the position and to seek a place to live. At the time, there were virtually no rentals and only a few houses on the market. Without consulting Sharon I made a decision to buy a house that was within a very short walk to the College. We were happy in the house.

We invited my sister Selma to allow her son Matthew, who was the same age as our son Douglas, to live with us that school year. She agreed and we had two 8-year old boys and one 2-year-old daughter for the year.

The boys walked to and from their elementary school, about a half-mile from home and just on the other side of the campus, often taking a short cut through the fields. On one day in January, it had been snowing throughout the day, but a predicted severe storm came quicker than anticipated. The wind quickly increased to gale force and the temperature began dropping rapidly on its way toward zero. I drove to school to pick up the boys but was a moment late. They had already started on their trek through waist high snowdrifts. What was a half-mile walk, could, for short legs, buffeting winds, and whiteout conditions, easily have become a multi-mile death march.

Running into the field I spotted them and had to actually touch them to get their attention as the wind drowned out my shouts.

"We can walk home!" they protested, totally oblivious to the danger they faced.

The storm was the first moment of a three-week period in which the temperature hovered between zero and thirty degrees below zero.

When we arrived home and the boys became aware of the severity of the storm, they had no cute sayings, but to this day they remember that storm with a degree of excitement.

We had just arrived in Dickinson when a great summer storm approached. I grabbed Douglas and we drove to the overpass at the western edge of town to be pelleted by huge raindrops and to experience the wind buffeting the car. Many other times in differing locales, Douglas and I stood or sat together to be buffeted by the weather and to enjoy nature's great force.

I soon learned the sound of a weather front. Think of a high-speed freight train bearing down on you. The noise of a front precedes the arrival of the winds. In the Great Plains there are no hills or forests to break up the noise and the front is free to loudly announce its arrival.

In the summer, I became an intent watcher of weather, as I needed to know conditions for our outdoor summer theatre and whether we should cancel a performance. One summer evening I observed a very tall and wide thunderstorm cell moving easterly, but fortunately ten miles north of our community. As the storm moved to the east and the evening skies darkened we became aware of the dozens of flashes of lightning, until at a point, the entire cell was as if it were illuminated from within. This thunderstorm cell, perhaps ten miles in diameter, and 60 thousand feet high, that night dropped ten inches of rain on a community not far from us. We, however, were totally free of rain or wind and the show went on.

As part of the Big Sky country Dickinson shares that region's clean, dry air. The lack of humidity reveals clouds that are never seen in the eastern parts of the country. We can see and study the great turbulence that marks the bottom of clouds during stormy weather. Clouds can move with great speed and great force. One feels humble in the presence of such great force.

One Saturday morning in downtown Dickinson, wearing a light jacket, I was surprised to see the bank's thermometer report a temperature of zero degrees Fahrenheit. The air was dry and the wind calm, accounting in part for feeling comfortable, but then we had just emerged from a three-week spell when the highest temperature was about 25 degrees below zero.

Driving an automobile in Dickinson in the winter would be very hazardous to anyone not used to having snow on the ground. There was little point for the city to clear the streets of snow because more was sure to follow. Winter temperatures never rose high enough to melt the snow, so we drove on snow packed streets and did so with few accidents. People drove slowly and carefully with snow tires, studded tires, or with wheel chains.

Our house on 8th Avenue had two furnaces. When previous owners had built an addition to house a master bedroom they installed a second furnace. During our cold spells our well-insulated house was always cozy and our utility bills were reasonable.

There are stories of farmhouses in which stout ropes were attached from the house to the barn so that farmers who had to milk their cows would not get lost during a snow blinding "white out."

Major highways were surprisingly clear most of the winter as the constant wind kept snow blowing across the road, not allowing it to stick and stay. "Inverse sublimation" is the process that allows snow to pass from its solid state directly into a gas without first melting. That is what happened to a great deal of North Dakota snow.

Western North Dakota is butte country. A butte is a conspicuous isolated hill with steep, often vertical sides and a small, relatively flat top. Once, I climbed a butte on a clear day and watched jet contrails begin on the western horizon and disappear on the eastern horizon. This is an hour-long flight and a distance of nearly 600 miles.

We took advantage of the interesting topography of this region visiting the North Dakota Badlands and the Theodore Roosevelt National Monument (now a National Park). I recall the two boys skipping rocks across the Missouri River, which at that point was only a stream. Douglas and I slept out in a clearing in the park on a moonless, clear night, falling asleep by counting the meteorites streaking across the night sky.

ARRIVING AT WRIGHT STATE UNIVERSITY

By the time I came to Wright State University in 1970, I had been a college professor for 10 years and had learned to handle pressure, to set goals, to work with my bosses and my colleagues.

When I came to Dayton in the winter of 1970 to interview for the position of Director of Theatre I was excited about the prospect of building a vibrant theatre program. The campus was sparkling new. The campus consisted of only four buildings—the Quad, four four-story rectangular buildings arranged around an inner court. However, the state had appropriated four million dollars to build a Creative Arts Center. To my way of thinking this was an ideal situation. Here was a new, developing state-supported University in a large metropolitan area in a great state. Of course I was happy about the prospect of returning to Ohio after ten years living west of the Mississippi. Our families were located within 75 miles of Dayton, and Sharon and I and our two children would be able to see them on a frequent basis.

I was told later that of the four persons brought to campus to interview, I had been the one with the greatest enthusiasm for the position. The position was offered and I accepted by early February; each month thereafter I flew to Dayton to be involved in the design of the Theatre portion of the Creative Arts Center. It is hard to express how exciting this was. I worked very closely with Fred Meyer, the department's Technical Director, whom I quickly came to respect. We worked well together and enjoyed each other's company.

I was in my early 40's and reasonably fit. Driving to work in the morning through the back streets of Beavercreek gave me 15 minutes to prepare my mind for the day's work. Five would have been enough. I was anxious to get to work. Besides teaching, directing and producing plays, and attending meetings, my priority those first three years was to help design and supervise the building of the Creative Arts Center's theatre.

I was new to creating a theatre building and there was much to learn. We had the architects to guide us and they hired a theatre consultant. Unfortunately, the lead architect who taught at Miami University took the year off, leaving the design to two junior colleagues. And the theatre consultant had a negative reputation. So much of the work that Fred and I did with regard to the design of the building was to counter or rectify the architects' and consultant's design decisions.

Much of our attention was directed to the audience's comfort. Fred was 6 feet 4 inches tall and I was 6 feet 1 inch. Our long legs made us very aware of how uncomfortable it was to sit in chairs in crowded aisles. We insisted from the beginning that the rows be spaced 40 inches apart. Since we had "stadium seating," that is, with no aisle except at the end of the row, the extra space allows patrons to enter and exit with relative ease.

A second consideration in audience comfort was the chair itself. Here I had personal experience in chairs at the Guthrie Theatre in Minneapolis, and I insisted on specifications that would favor the American Seating Company. We did have samples from four companies, which we kept for several months, asking everyone to give their opinions. When the bids went out, we discovered that the building's general contractor had switched seats favoring another company. This was resolved by dealing directly with the general contractor.

A third audience consideration was the viewing angle. As the architects presented a new iteration of the auditorium, Fred and I would take out our straight edges and check the sight lines. Once the architects presented a plan in which an audience member siting in the balcony could not fully see an actor who stood downstage. Although the auditorium had fewer than 400 seats, the architect said that we could simply refrain from selling affected seats when that was a problem. He also said we would probably never sell out a production.

A fourth auditorium consideration was the height of the stage relative to the first row of seats. In the 19th century, 48 inches or more was standard. That would not be acceptable to our audiences in the rows closer to the stage that would be forced to sit looking up at a steep angle.

We had great difficulty forcing the architects to make the adjustments we wanted. The *coup de gras* came when, for "aesthetic reasons," the architects wished to have a great curve on the exterior wall of the scene house. "You don't understand" one said, "This is the main entrance." The problem was that a considerable portion of the stage would have been rendered unusable.

It was now at the end of the fall quarter in the second year of design work. Fred and I prepared a detailed critique of the design faults, which we presented to the architects. Our conclusion was that the current building design must be abandoned and the process started anew. This was a drastic suggestion and the architects must indeed have been upset.

At the next meeting a few weeks later, the knowledge of the problem had become known. Fred White, our acting President, was at the meeting, and after a few minutes, he informed the architects that they must "satisfy the user." He said it quietly but firmly. The architects asked what changes would satisfy us. We proceeded to tell them, and the changes were made.

The construction was exceedingly slow. Once, when a large, heavy electrical board was being installed on stage, the chain hoisting the board snapped, severely damaging the equipment when it fell to the floor. This accident paralyzed the electricians. They spent the next month playing poker.

Any new building, perhaps all new buildings, has design and construction problems. This was certainly true for the Creative Arts Center, and many of the following problems persisted for years.

- Noisy transformers that could be heard in the auditorium;
- Leaky skylights;
- Un-insulated tin covers for stage exhaust fans that acted as drums during rains;
- An unpaved exit from the commons to the parking lot that caused a lawsuit when a patron fell and broke her leg;
- Stage lifts that were below ground water level that became flooded; and
- Sound systems that did not function.

At the same time that we were dealing with the design and construction of the building, we were building curriculum, teaching classes, and directing and producing plays in a temporary building off campus. In spite of the immense pressure, we began attracting a coterie of talented and intelligent students. We worked them hard and they responded. There was an excitement in our department. Opportunities were there for the students, and a great opportunity was there for the Department and for the Theatre program.

A traveler on a train once asked the Conductor if they could smoke and he said no. "But those people are smoking." the traveler said. The conductor replied, "they didn't ask." That was a guiding principle for me. Our university administration was under pressure, things were chaotic, control was loose, and opportunity abounded.

EIGHTEEN WONDERFUL YEARS
At Wright State University
1970-1988

*An interview conducted by Professor Lewis Shoup and myself is available
online at the Wright State University Digital Archives, both in written and
auditory form. To hear or read the interview, go to
http://core.libraries.wright.edu/handle/2374.WSU/3692*

Eighteen years in a single work environment produces
many memorable highlights. In this abbreviated account
I would like to describe some of the highlights of my years at
Wright State University from 1970 through 1988.

The enthusiasm for coming to Wright State expressed in
the previous story remained boundless for all of my years at
the University. I recall leaving home in the morning always
looking forward to getting to work in the office. The standard
teaching load was three courses or nine hours each quarter
with a three-hour reduction for major responsibilities, such
as being a director of plays, or being an administrative head
of a department or other unit. I could have easily asked for a
further reduction of responsibilities because an eighty-hour
workweek was the norm.

When I arrived on campus I learned that the space where
plays had been presented previously would be available only
on the weekends. There would be no time for setting up a stage
or for rehearsal. It was therefore necessary, in the summer of
1970, before I was a paid faculty member, to begin searching
for an alternative performance space. My colleague Fred
Meyers, the theatre technical director, and I spent weeks
searching. We bid on an unused church in the Oregon Village
in downtown Dayton, but were turned down by the church's

board of directors. Finally we located a small hall—a grange
hall—on National Road, about one mile from the University.
We were able to rent the space for three weeks for each of the
six plays that we produced the first year. We had one week to
set up the stage and conduct final rehearsals, and two weeks
for performance. We named this found space "The New Liberty
Theatre."

We were obliged for the first production to install heavy-
duty electrical service, to build a gridiron of pipes from which
to hang the lighting instruments, to build a stage, to install
seating bleachers for the audience and a changing room for the
actors, and to transport scenery from campus. After the last of
six nights of performance, we dismantled the entire theatrical
set and all the supporting paraphernalia and transported it
back to the University for storage. We did this six times in the
first year, having increased the number of our productions from
three to six.

What an insane thing to do! But we were young and
enthusiastic and because of our audacious plan we attracted a
coterie of enthusiastic students. We were at the beginning of
something new and exciting and the students bought into that
vision.

While the new building, now called the Creative Arts
Center, was being designed, we continued producing plays in
the New Liberty Theatre except for the last play of the third
season. We decided to put Shakespeare's *The Taming of the
Shrew* outdoors on the Quad—that is, on the green lawn
between the four existing buildings. Again, it was a makeshift
operation. We had to arrange for heavy-duty electrical service.
Even more difficult to accomplish, the very noisy air blowers on
the roof of each of the four buildings had to be turned off during
the two-hour presentation of the play. But the excitement for
the production by the students and audience was palpable.
We had a very large cast. The play was presented on a raked

stage in Italian renaissance costumes. I directed the play and was extremely fortunate to have an eighteen-year old highly talented freshman student play the lead role of Katherine and an equally highly talented young man to play Petruchio. They were the glue around which the production was built. Other student actors found the prospect of Shakespeare in an outdoor setting enticing and exciting. I assigned one student the task of creating a Renaissance style pre-show show with musicians, singers, dancers, street vendors, and more.

At the end of the first week of *The Shrew*, on a Saturday night, a spring storm caused the entire set to collapse. No flats were left standing. Only the stage platform remained. I told Fred, our technical director, there was no need to rebuild the set. We would play on a bare stage.

Unbeknownst to me, the students made a decision to rebuild the set. Wendell Meier was the student who was most instrumental in causing the set to be re-erected. He worked through several nights to make this possible. Many other actors and technicians joined Wendell in this project. What this incident did for the morale of our department cannot be over estimated.

We had enthusiastic and intelligent students who could have gone to school at other colleges but stayed at Wright State because they sensed the excitement and the opportunities to perform in plays and to design sets and costumes in a supportive atmosphere. For many years following the production, audience members would say they remembered the play and how much fun they had.

. . . . .

In 1971, I attended the convention of the American Educational Theatre Association in San Francisco. There I met John Walker, Chairman of the Theatre Department at Ohio State University. I knew John because he had hired me to direct two plays for the 1964 Ohio University Summer

Theatre when he was chairman there. Our conversations centered on the establishment of a statewide education theatre organization. John was well known and respected throughout the state. When he sent a letter inviting department chairs to participate in the formation of a statewide organization a good number of people responded.

At that meeting, I was one of five persons elected to be on the committee to draft a constitution. We met at Ohio State University several times and I got to know the members very well. More importantly I learned a great deal about leadership, from seasoned professionals including John Walker, Al Kaufman, (Ohio University,) Don Rosenberg, (Miami University). The committee finished its work and another general meeting accepted the constitution of the Ohio Theatre Alliance. I was elected Treasurer. One of my theatre faculty became Newsletter Editor, and the University's graphic artist designed the OTA logo.

Wright State University, the state's newest and youngest institution was suddenly known around the state. For myself, I had the opportunity to meet colleagues, to learn what directions other programs were taking, what new ideas were viable.

The word "mentor" and "mentoring" was not in vogue in the early 1970's, but the OTA in many respects became my personal mentor. It was very instructive to learn how others dealt with thorny problems, whether it be childish-acting faculty or overbearing superiors. I learned from them how they built audiences, and how they found professional actors, speakers, and designers.

The dedication of the Creative Arts Center was as festive an occasion as we could make it. Our president, Robert Keggereis was put out that we had not invited the architects and we received some criticism for inviting a lot of theatre people from around the state. However, the fact that we received virtually no help in planning the dedication is an indication that the University was in a novice state. A few years later there would have been an office that would have taken charge and invited the "friends of the University." At this time, we knew very few important people in the greater Dayton community.

We named our main performance space "The Festival Playhouse," and our smaller experimental space "The Celebration Theatre." Our naming of these spaces angered the University Provost, Andrew Spiegel, because he didn't know about it in advance. Our philosophy was never to ask first if we could do something, but to do it, and receive a rebuke if it came.

The Festival Playhouse was a beautiful and wonderfully functional performance space both for audience comfort and for the production of plays. We had just fewer than 400 seats including three rows in the balcony. We could say that there was not a single bad seat in the house. We had carefully chosen seats manufactured by the American Seating Company, considered at the time as the cream of the crop. When the building contractor surreptitiously tried to substitute a lesser grade seats, our strenuous objections caused his retreat.

. . . . .

Having a nice theatre and having established a positive reputation in the state, I was visited by two faculty from the American College Theatre Festival asking if we would host the next Festival in the winter of 1977. When the theatre faculty agreed, saying this would be a good thing for our students and for the department, we accepted the invitation and the challenge.

Six colleges were selected to send their productions to be presented on our Festival Playhouse stage. Following each of the performances, a trio of professional judges critiqued the play and the performances. This was a great learning experience for the performers and for the audience of students and faculty. The performances were strictly noncompetitive. Students from the five schools not performing were enthusiastic and intelligent audiences who caught the subtleties of language and action.

We were asked to sponsor the Festival a second year, and this we did. The second year was as successful as the first, if not more so. From this point further, our reputation had been established in the state, but not in the University.

There existed in the College of Liberal Arts antagonism toward the arts and Theatre Arts in particular because it was assumed that we have been give an extra favorable status and received greater support than deserved. Nothing could have been further from the truth. We were grossly understaffed (nine faculty at one point). We were a profit center for the University as our rate of reimbursement from the state was the highest for an undergraduate program.

The Ohio Board of Higher Education initiated a program to recognize outstanding programs in the state and to make substantive financial grants. We applied for an Academic Excellence Award in 1982 and were granted it receiving a $150,000 award, a very substantial amount of money. We were the only Wright State program so recognized. Two years later we were again given a Program Excellence Award with an even bigger grant. A third state award was later granted to our Motion Pictures program as recognition for its excellence. In a five-year period, our department was recognized three times as among the most excellent programs in the state. No other single department in the entire state had been so honored!

Motion Pictures had been started in the University Library because the then director knew that printed materials would have less value in the future, and that the computer and digital files would become more important. However, after two years, they recognized that the teaching of Motion Pictures constituted more trouble than they were willing to have and asked Liberal Arts to take over the program. Dean Cantelupe asked if Theatre would be willing to take over the program and our answer was an immediate and emphatic yes.

A year later, the Music Department decided that teaching dance was a greater burden than they wished to have. We again said yes when we were asked to absorb Dance. We thus became the Department of Theatre Arts with studies in Theatre, Motion Pictures and Dance.

Having a supportive boss for eleven years is what allowed us to grow and prosper. We grew because he wanted the departments in the college to thrive. When I came to him saying the time had come for us to establish a BFA (Bachelor of Fine Arts) degree he agreed. But when I said that if I had to go through all the College and University committees and then through the Board of Regents at the state level, it would take three years. He looked at me and said to just put it in the new catalogue. And we did. And the next catalog also saw the change of the Department of Art into the Department of Art and Art History, again with no approval from any committee. He knew that the purpose of review committees in the University was to slow down initiatives and new programs. We were thus able to leap frog most of the other undergraduate programs in Ohio.

The real secret to growth in academia is having the right leader. Charles Derry was the faculty person who coordinated Motion Pictures. He was a brilliant scholar, teacher and creative artist.

The Dance Program struggled until I was able to hire three new instructors simultaneously. At the beginning of the academic year, before classes began, we met at my house for several days in order to construct a totally new dance curriculum. Kathy (Suzanne) Walker became the coordinator of Dance. She was a superb teacher and choreographer and a hard and dedicated worker. The dance program began to thrive with her leadership. I had been serving on the Board of the

Dayton Ballet and its Artistic Director, Stuart Sebastian, first led me to Suzanne, and then to Mary Giannone, a petite, fiery choreographer and teacher. With the third faculty member, Sandra Tanner, we suddenly had a strong faculty upon which to build the dance program.

There was in the department an employee with the title of "Business Manager," a title that the University could understand and approve, but one that is a grave misnomer. The persons who served in this position were (choose your title) Publicist, Newspaper Writer, Editor and Publisher, Box Office Supervisor, Administrative Assistant, Trouble Shooter, Conceptualizer, sometimes Acting Chair, and Confidant.

Serving in this position were three most remarkable young persons who were essential contributors to our successes. They were:

- David Heath, who moved to New York to test the theatrical waters, taking a temporary job at CBS News. His high competency and positive personality lead to a succession of promotions at CBS, and eventually into book publishing in St. Paul, Minnesota.
- Jim Volz, who left for graduate studies, gained his doctorate, and became Managing Director at the Alabama Shakespeare Festival. He then formed his own Arts Consultancy firm and became a full professor at Fullerton State University in California.
- Patti Russo, who left to earn an MFA degree in Creative Writing, and was hired by Borders Books, rising to management level. She is now a lecturer in the Ross School of Business at the University of Michigan, and is the Director of their part time MBA program.

Each of these three lovely people possessed superior writing skills and that may be the single quality that propelled them upward on their careers. Ironically, all three married spouses who were students in the Department of Theatre Arts, which attests to the high quality of our students!

. . . . .

There is one more thing I would like to say about building the department, something that was unique in the University. No other department in the University recruited students with the vigor and consistency we had. We began recruiting students from the very first year. We were in constant contact with high schools, working to be known to their drama teachers. Our reach eventually extended throughout the state and then outside the state. After the BFA had been in existence a few years, we were able to require auditions for admittance to the program, thereby raising the quality of our students. Soon after, Dance and Motion Pictures also began requiring auditions.

There is much more one could write about those 18 years; however, this is not a history of the department but rather a recounting of some highlights. One could talk about the awards the motion picture students began accruing, the dance students who went on to a professional career, and the many fine theatre productions and the way in which we soon had sell-out seasons, despite the architect's assertion that we wouldn't need all the seats in the auditorium.

In concluding, I must say that our success was possible only because we were able to attract excellent faculty and staff, and importantly, highly talented students.

VI | THOUGHTS

STEPPING FORWORD

I often lunch with former colleagues who call ourselves the ROMEO group---Retired Old Men Eating Out. Today, at Panera Breads, we crowded around three small round tables, making it difficult for some to leave their seats until everyone rose. My seat, however, afforded an easy exit. At the end of the meal, I took my tray to the nearby trash area and then began clearing my colleagues' trays.

Later in the day, a thought came to me for the first time. A personal characteristic I think I have possessed all my life, but never articulated before, regards this simple truth: I have always been interested in achieving a small step that would improve myself or my environment. In other words I would say that I like to fix things that need fixing, are capable of being fixed and will produce value on being fixed.

During my junior year at college I participated in Bowling Green University's Huron Playhouse summer theatre. Meals were served in the school cafeteria. When I noticed that the array of utensils and dishes were illogically placed, I re-ordered them into a more useful pattern. I would not have remembered this incident except that Professor Smith's wife Betty made a comment about Abe's penchant for orderliness.

If I see a situation where components are out of order, I desire to re-order them, to improve them, to make them function more efficiently, with less effort, and with greater productivity. Accomplishing the next possible step is satisfying.

I enjoyed the responsibility that came with being the "director of broadcasting" in my first job and later the head of a theatre program. Such situations always present one with the challenge of fixing problems to make them work better.

Administrators seem to delight in asking for five-year strategic plans, an idea seemingly borrowed from the Communist Soviet Union. There are sometimes more efficient ways to move forward and that is one step at a time with each step forward based on the step that came before.

Doing what CAN be done led, I believe, to developing what arguably became the best exclusively undergraduate theatre program in Ohio and in the Midwest. The central vision was to do what was possible, logical, and productive.

WORKING

How fortunate it is that I always enjoyed working. Where did my own love of work come from? Does one inherit this trait? As a young person, I recall seeing my father hard at work, and thinking I did not want to follow in his footsteps. I didn't understand the satisfaction that comes from being successful in your work or the satisfaction of being able to provide for your family.

Had I been the oldest child in the family and not the youngest, working with my father in the confectionary store or restaurant would probably have been my destiny. Without question my sisters' lives would have been much different, as they would not have been obligated to devote themselves to working in the confectionary store. They would have been freer to seek their own destiny. But as the junior child in the family, my father, wisely, nodded his assent to allow me to study what was at 16 years of age my passion.

Before marriage, I was content to work for daily subsistence, and my needs were minimal affording me time to pursue my interests. After marriage and the birth of my son, I became conscious of the need to earn money to support my family. However, I was never motivated to seek a position based solely on the amount of money paid. If that had been the case, I would not have become a teacher. My philosophy was that if one enjoys his work, he will work hard, and if he works well, he will be fairly compensated. Added compensation generally follows added responsibility, which follows hard work and success in the previous position. In my career, I never accepted a position that did not increase my compensation from the previous job, but it was always the added responsibility that excited me.

In my first years of work, there certainly was a time when I felt compensation was not adequate to our needs. We lived hand-to-mouth, with our income very carefully allotted to our needs. Still, we managed. We never carried great debt and never went hungry. We never failed to pay our rent or doctor bills; we lived a frugal but fruitful and happy life.

When we came to Wright State University in 1970, I was 39 years old. All my worldly possessions came with me in a 24-foot U-Haul truck. I had only $3,000 in assets, but importantly, no debt. At this point in their careers, many of my high school classmates were well established in their businesses and careers, and some were getting ready to send children to college.

Now, my son Douglas loves his work, and he works very hard, which he often tells me, as if he were the first to learn about hard work. Did he inherit this from me or from Sharon, who also was a very hard worker? Probably not. I suspect that people who are hard workers are people who are doing something they enjoy doing. And it doesn't hurt to live in a country where one can become educated and where social class is not an impediment to self-improvement.

As a professor I always encouraged young people to follow their instincts and their love, and I encourage parents to allow their children this freedom. Freedom is the key, hard work is the price one pays for loving what they do, and self-worth is the result of accomplishment. Joy of living is the goal we desire. This is the essence of good.

FOLLOW YOUR HEART, HANNAH

A letter to my grand niece on her graduation from college with a major in dance.

I congratulate you on your artistic bent, your graduation from college, and your *cum laude* honors! That is super, really super! I am so proud of you. I have always admired and gravitated toward artistic people and toward bright people. You are the light and I am the moth.

Where does your artistic bent come from? Well, it is in your genes and it was honed with art and music in your home. I got mine, very clearly from my Mama Rahija, who taught herself to play the piano, and from her singing, and from all of my sisters who could play musical instruments; and from my Uncle Jasper, the artistic photographer. It runs in our family, and I am glad it is still running.

I played the trombone and took piano and drum lessons and sang in the Glee Club and A Capella Choir and listened endlessly to musical comedy and classical music.

In 1940 (I was 10) my father bought a large, floor model Zenith AF FM radio, which contained a 78-rpm automatic record changer. Your grandmother purchased a multi-disc record album of Tchaikovsky's Fifth Symphony. There is a particularly exciting passage in the 5th that features the trombone section. I heard that passage dozens of times and found it as thrilling the last time as the first. Little did I know how those moments would probably shape my life. Whatever it was, it resonated profoundly.

When I was a high school junior I decided I wanted to study "Radio Speech" in college. I told Papa of my desire. He didn't say much at first because I am sure he wanted me to study business and come home to run the confectionary. At some point in the first semester at college, he blessed my choice of major, seeing and appreciating my enthusiasm. He died during my second semester of college so I am eternally grateful for his approval.

Why am I telling you this story? Because I feel very strongly that a person should study what they feel is right for them. They should follow their heart, their gut instincts. It is the same way with all of life's really important decisions. Whenever a student came to tell me they had decided to change their major from theatre to another subject, my response was always: "Congratulations, you have made a valuable and important discovery for yourself. You are doing the right thing. I wish you well."

When I graduated from college and finished my term in the army, I came to San Francisco to get a job in business. I had a great time in The City, but I discovered that I didn't want to work in a corporation. I had no friends who were happy in their work. I wanted a job I could commit to—a job that met my needs to learn, to grow, to contribute, to be fulfilled. To hell with money, who needs it? I grew up without money, learned to have fun without money, got married without money, and who needed it anyway. Follow my heart. That was one of the most important insights of my life.

When I chose to study Radio Speech, I had no clue where it would lead. It was six years later when I decided I wanted to become a teacher. I was married and nearly 29 years old before I stepped into a classroom to test my desire.

Well, Hannah, where will your love of dance lead? Who knows? Who cares? It will lead where it leads and take you along. There will be choices to be made, and they may at the time be startling choices, seemingly jumping to the right and then to the left, and maybe, once or twice, seemingly backwards. But when you are in your fifties, more or less, and you look back on those choices, the path will be remarkably straight.

You will understand that where you are, at that moment, you were destined to be. It will have been a happy journey. You will be a happy, fulfilled human being.

So I congratulate you on your totally unsafe and unpredictable choice, I welcome you into the artistic side of our family, and I charge you, in time, with the responsibility of passing your love on to the next generation(s).

With love, Uncle Abe

ON MARRIAGE

I was given the great honor of officiating the wedding of my grand niece Jane Rutherdale to Jesse Ward-Karet, June 23, 2012. In order to do so, I was ordained by the Universal Life Church.

Welcome everyone! Here we are at about 7140 feet above sea level to celebrate (finally!) the marriage of Jane and Jesse. Allow me to introduce myself. My name is Abe Bassett and I am Jane's great-uncle, brother of her maternal grandmother.

I'd like to start by thanking you on behalf of Jesse and Jane for trekking all the way up here, dirt road and all! Jane and Jesse chose to hold their wedding in the Sierra Nevada because it is an area to which they both feel a strong connection. Jesse's love of the Sierras developed though snowboarding, so he particularly enjoys the crags and steep valleys of the area. Jane grew up spending summers sailing and swimming in Lake Tahoe and hiking in the surrounding mountains.

As many of you may know, Jesse and Jane first met in the spring of 2002, when Jane and her college roommate answered an advertisement for a room in Jesse's apartment. It wasn't until the beginning of the following year however, after living together for a semester, that Jane and Jesse started dating. Their relationship must have developed by spring though . . .as Jane's father relates, "I knew it was getting serious when Jesse showed up in Redwood City for one of Jane's crew races!"

Of course I have known Jane all of her life. I first met Jesse at a family dinner that my wife and I hosted at a Chinese restaurant in San Francisco. Apparently I made quite an impression because the couple still laughs today about the incident. Being the smart aleck that I am, I asked Jesse in front of all the assembled family members, "What are your intentions, young man?" Fortunately Jesse has a great sense of humor and saw the joke for what is was—mostly teasing. Now, as I stand before you to perform this marriage, I can affirm that Jesse's intentions were (and are) entirely honorable.

I have some standing in talking about longevity in marriage because last Wednesday, June 20, my wife Sharon and I celebrated the 53rd anniversary of our wedding. The longevity belongs mainly to the quality of "stick-to-it-tivness" that my wife brought to the marriage: She said that if I were ever to leave her, she was coming with me.

A wedding ceremony is not unlike a graduation exercise. It is a commencement with advice to the graduates. The long tradition of wedded folks giving advice to newly weds, is akin a message in a bottle, cast adrift in the hopes someone will open it. To the newly wed, I once simplified my advice to a four-letter word: "t-a-l-k". But I came to see there is a much more important word in maintaining a good relationship. "Talk" is good but the better concept is "Listen". The Greek philosopher Epictetus reminds us "Nature gave us one tongue and two ears so we could hear twice as much as we speak." And Oscar Wilde tells us that the "ultimate bond of all companionship, whether in marriage or in friendship, is conversation."

Jane and Jesse are intelligent, mature, strong, still young people who have known each other for nearly a decade. They know each other well. And they know that all marriages have their rough spots and difficult times. The perfect marriage is a work of fiction. All enduring relationships have undergone a continuing process of renewal. A lasting relationship comes because two people have worked hard at understanding their partner. It is only then they can smooth and refresh their relationship. Listening to your partner is the foundation.

Listening is what allows you to know your partner.

William Butler Yates said that a long life together with all its accidents is barely enough time for a man and woman to understand each other, and to understand is to love. And Ruth Bell Graham says that a good marriage is the union of two good forgivers. And lets not forget Goethe who claims it is essential for a husband and wife to quarrel because that is how they get to know each other. And it doesn't hurt for a quarreling couple to remember they are on the same side.

Now, Jesse, if these words are discouraging to you, remember the advice Socrates gave to a young man. He said get married. If you find a good wife you'll be happy. If not, you'll become a philosopher. Jesse, you have chosen well, (or been well chosen). You have no prospect of becoming a philosopher.

VIOLENCE IN IRAQ

Whether fictional or real, I hate violence. There is no thrill in movies watching bombs blowing buildings to "smithereens," to use the phrase that so delighted us as children. Movies with exploding automobiles may thrill a teenager but not the adult I have become.

These thoughts on violence are prompted by the American invasion of Iraq. I can barely stand to watch the news, and as a matter of fact, I haven't watched 15 minutes today. I pass on the newspaper stories; the headlines tell me all I want or need to know.

Pictures of exploding buildings in Baghdad do not thrill. Who were the grown men with little boy's minds who thought of the phrase "shock and awe?" Was the phrase describing the initial bombing campaign of the Iraqi war meant to frighten the Iraqis or impress upon the American populace the might of our military?

I don't hate Iraqis whether civilians or soldiers. I do not see them as demons. They are people like my neighbors and me. They want to feed and nourish their children. They want their children to have better lives than they enjoy. It may be okay to hurt Saddam, but not the children and their mothers, nor the old women and old men, or innocent bystanders. Not even the young people who find themselves in the military, those who are easily indoctrinated, those who welcome war, those who have yet to see people burned, maimed and killed. These horrible images have yet to be burned into their consciousness.

Those who have had violence visited upon them had their views sharply shaped from that moment. For me, it was an accumulative awareness that took time before I could say aloud, "I hate violence." Having said it, images of the past—the carnage of the Civil War, Southern lynchings, concentration camps—have new potency and meaning.

This war in Iraq is so wrong, so stupid, so hurtful and the repercussions will last for decades. This is not the America I grew up in and love. Nor the America that I was proud to serve as a young Army recruit. Not the America that espouses justice and freedom for all. I have always been aware of our many faults, but until now, I thought we had it under control and things would improve.

A TV report last night had the audacity to label an Iraqi maneuver as "ingenious." Can you imagine that word being attached to a "third world" nation? Ingenuity is an American invention. How dare these foreigners be ingenious? And how dare they fight back and defend their country. Haven't they read our press clippings, aren't they watching CNN? Won't they pay attention to the talking heads boasting of our power? Don't they know they are supposed to surrender, ignore their leaders, and rebel against the regime? How dare they make us send our boys home in body bags?

What has changed is that when I was younger, I thought the world was on an upward path of improvement. I thought we would learn from our past and grow toward good sense and love and tranquility. Now, in the second decade of the 21st century, we still hear talk of using the military to solve problems.

When will the good news come? How will we know it when it does come? Will it make us happy? Will America ever again be a beacon to the world?

CHURCHES, CATHEDRALS, MOSQUES AND MUSIC

In Fort Wayne, Indiana, the First Presbyterian Church sponsored a community theatre in their church with a dedicated facility that many Little Theatres would be proud to own. Remarkably, the plays were never censored. The paid Artistic Director could produce whatever plays he deemed of interest to the audience. There were some plays one would never expect to see in a church-sponsored theatre. I was very impressed with their liberal attitude. If I wished to be a regular churchgoer, I would select Fort Wayne's First Presbyterian Church.

Interestingly, I had a second cousin whose family was Presbyterian. Sometime in the 19th century, a young man came to the village of Kfeir, Lebanon. He asked for food and a place to stay as he was without resources. Six months later, when he departed the village, several families had been converted to Presbyterianism.

Technically, I am an Episcopalian because I was baptized and confirmed in that church. When I was a student at Bowling Green I went to an Episcopalian service one Sunday, and the student-parishioners were calling the pastor, "Father". That was the first time I knew that there was a "high" Episcopal Church, closely related in ritual to the Catholic Church. The Episcopal Church in West Virginia was decidedly a "low" Episcopal Church.

The next time I went to a church service of my own free will was in Liverpool, England. Stuck in this northwestern industrial city, I was looking for an opportunity to work my way home on a freighter. I was lonesome and hoped I could meet some people. The Sunday experience did not meet my wishes, and that was that.

Not counting funerals and weddings, visits to churches and mosques have been infrequent except during our travels. We visited major cathedrals in many places to marvel at their history and their exceptional architecture. St. Peters in Rome, the Duomo of Milano, St. Paul's and Westminster Abbey in London, Notre Dame in Paris are truly exceptional.

Cathedrals and churches are also exceptional as venues for music. The voices and sounds of the Boys Choir in Westminster Abbey during Evensong will always remain in my consciousness. The organ recitals in Grace Cathedral in San Francisco, and the chamber music programs in St. Martin's in The Field in London are memorable. Some musical venues are successfully held in small churches such as the Yellow Springs (Ohio) First Presbyterian Church, home to a very successful chamber music series. In Sacramento, the Westminster Presbyterian Church's beautiful Byzantine-Romanesque sanctuary is home to a weekly noontime concert.

Among Mosques, I can't image a more beautiful structure than the Dome of the Rock on the Temple Mount in the Old City of Jerusalem.

On our travels, our guides always led us to the most interesting churches. In Iceland, we came across a neat and well-maintained church that would accommodate only a dozen parishioners.

The Williamson West Virginia Episcopal Church of my youth reportedly had been brought over the mountains in sections to be erected on a small plot of land. I can still picture the dozen rows of pews and the open ceiling. It was a humble place, decidedly appropriate for a "low" Episcopal Church.

MY MUSICAL LIFE

Like bread and butter, music and youth go together, judging by the huge number of young people walking in step with their iPods, shaking their heads and bodies in rhythm to their automobile radios, tapping their fingers to tunes that run through their heads. Strange behavior indeed, except that I was once a young person doing the same. Music was and remains an important part of my life.

My mother taught herself to read music and to play the piano and all my older sisters had musical training. They played the piano, of course, but also the mandolin, tuba, French horn, clarinet, and other instruments. The first music that caught my attention, other than music I may have heard in my mother's womb, was that of the Williamson High School Marching Band. I was nearly three and under the watchful eye of my mother as I ran to the front porch to watch the band march by our house. The rat-ta-ta-tat of the snare drums and boom-boom of the base drum excited me and awakened my senses.

Just before World War II broke out, the improving economy meant there was money in the family for some luxury items. My father purchased a Zenith floor model AM-FM radio with a 78-rpm record player. One of my sisters had purchased an album of Tchaikovsky's Fifth Symphony. There is a passage in the third movement where, in building toward one of the many climaxes, the trombones were heavily involved. Because I was learning to play the trombone, the thrill of this passage caused me to play the album endlessly over and over.

As I entered Junior High School I joined the band—my sister Selma was the Band Director—playing the trombone.

The trombone section consisted of two players, Charles Horn and me. (That was the same Charles Horn, who during marching drills, managed to "accidentally" step on my trombone slides.) In John Phillip Sousa's *Semper Fidelis*, there is a short but difficult passage that requires the trombone section to not only play the correct notes, but to do it with perfect timing. We were so proud, when, finally, after more than a few tries, the trombone passage was executed perfectly.

My first musical instrument was the drums, but all I had with which to practice were two drumsticks and one rubber drum pad, a great saver of my parents' money and sanity. Someone showed me how to hold the drumsticks, but that was all. I had a few piano lessons while in elementary school, but I never progressed very far beyond reading music, not by the notes, but by the numbers that floated above the notes. "Every Good Boy Does Fine"– E G B D F–helped me remember the notes of the treble clef. Eventually, as a trombonist, I became at home with the bass clef. I played in the band for four years and became reasonably adept.

I don't know when I first started creating tunes, but melodies were always running through my head and taking form through my lips. I never wrote words to the music, but the music flowed effortlessly and constantly.

During college with the advent of the LP record, my musical world changed. I purchased a few recordings but with my various roommates there was always music to be played. A few days ago, I heard strains of Dvořák's New World Symphony, and a rush of feeling took me back to my college days. The music that thrilled me in this, the first stage of serious musical appreciation, were the symphonies of the Romantic period: Tchaikovsky, Dvořák, Grieg, Rachmaninoff, Beethoven, etc.

There were two seminal events that furthered my love of classical music. After the Army while living in San Francisco, I attended a performance of the San Francisco Symphony

Orchestra. I had purchased an inexpensive ticket, which placed me in the second balcony, where I literally looked down on the orchestra. The main piece that evening was Ravel's *La Valse*, which with its ever-changing rhythm was hypnotic, especially for one being introduced to the work. During the performance the orchestra transformed itself from a group of black-clad musicians, into an organic being. The arms of the violinists swung in unison and their torsos came to and fro as they bowed in unison to the undulating rhythm. It was a transformational experience that carried me away.

One year later, a second musical event may also be termed transformational. The experience occurred in Paris. Students were allowed to purchase last minute tickets at very low prices. You often happily discovered your seats were in the most expensive sections of the auditorium. On this occasion, I had come to a chamber music concert. It was serendipitous that my first chamber concert should be a performance by the young Amadeus Quartet, a superb group still in worldwide performance. They performed that night Franz Schubert's *La Jeune Fille et la Mort*—Death and the Maiden—a rich, dramatic, melodic work. I was greatly moved. I had never had a more wonderful musical experience. What an incredible way to be introduced to chamber music. To this day, I would rather listen to string quartets than any other music.

If I were to be isolated on an island and could have my choice of music, it would be the string quartets of Mozart, Beethoven, Haydn, and Vivaldi. Chamber music is far less likely to wear out its welcome on repeated hearings. Aaron Copland, in his book on the appreciation of music—*What to Listen For in Music*—wrote that great music could bear repetition while lesser music cannot. That, he explains, is why popular music has such a relatively short life.

But lest you think I am one dimensional, you should know that I have broader musical tastes. I missed the Beatles revolution as it occurred, but a few years ago, I bought an album of Beatles hits, discovering their music was pretty good—good melodies, good rhythms, good lyrics. I listened to that album six or seven times before it wore out its welcome. The same thing happened when I discovered the tenor voice and plaintive folk songs of John Denver. Recently the movie, *Walk The Line*, about the life of Johnny Cash, made me cognizant of the pleasing and interesting music of this bass-voiced country music artist.

I grew up with the music of the great Broadway musicals. When I was young, I wondered if the music of Rogers and Hammerstein would ever be surpassed. And I have continued to enjoy music of the musical theatre, and on Saturdays I often listen to portions of the opera broadcast. A few weeks ago, I traveled into the hills of Eastern Kentucky where the radio station with the strongest signal played without interruption the music of the hills: a conglomerate of country, blues, blue grass, hillbilly, gospel and Irish. When I was a very young person I made the observation that the people of the hills enjoyed music we more sophisticated people thought was noise. I could never again make such an arrogant assertion.

Musical arrogance comes with being young. In Okinawa, my civilian friend George Kilmer told me he did not like the music of George Gershwin. My response, the next time I was invited to dinner, was to bring him a LP recording of *Rhapsody in Blue*. How could anything so lovely not be loved by anyone, if they would only listen, or so I thought at the time? Musical arrogance is what makes young people open the windows of their homes and cars so their neighbors can hear their beautiful music.

Music has given me untold pleasure, as it has to most people. And while I do not carry a Boom Box, a Walkman, or an iPod, and while invented melodies no longer flow freely from my head or heart . . . I can hardly imagine a world without music.

A WAKE UP CALL

Saturday, September 5, 2009, was the perfect day for football. My nephew Mitchell and I enjoyed the Ohio State vs. Navy game, which Ohio State won, but almost lost. We met at the bookstore on 11th Avenue and High Street to have a sandwich before walking through campus to Ohio Stadium. After the game we chose to again walk through campus to the Happy Greek Restaurant for a snack of Greek food that was very similar to Lebanese food. We had done this the previous year, and Mitch so enjoyed the food that he subsequently brought his family to the restaurant.

By the time we left the restaurant the football traffic had subsided, and getting on Interstate 71 was easy. The one glass of Greek ale that accompanied my light meal may have contributed to a feeling of sleepiness, as did my habit of rising early in the morning. Aware of the oncoming drowsiness, I intended to pull into the rest stop that was unfortunately another fifteen miles south.

I don't recall shutting my eyes or nodding or hearing the roar of tires crossing the warning barrier on the left shoulder of the highway. My car had moved from the outside lane to the median strip before my eyes came to high alert and my brain could assess the situation. Holding tight to the steering wheel, I did not over compensate as I steered the car back toward the pavement. The car jerked and started to skid as the tires on the right were on the pavement and the tires on the left still on the grass.

The heavy dose of adrenaline coursing though my system disposed of the sleepiness I had earlier suffered. There was no need to visit the rest stop, although I did buy an ice cream fudge bar at the next convenience store.

Thinking back on this incident made me realized how lucky I was. There were no other vehicles immediately in front, behind me or to the side of me, during the time I lost consciousness or during my return to the highway. In this section of the median strip there were no signposts or sewer culverts, no overpass with guardrails. The slope into the median was gradual and the bottom of the median strip was smooth, much more like a gentle U than a sharp V. As I continued on my way I observed how many impediments were in the median strip and how any one of them could have been lethal to an automobile traveling at 65 miles per hour.

A few days later, on two consecutive days, there were traffic deaths on the freeway near our house. In both cases, the drivers, both of whom were young, over-corrected their swerving vehicles that had slipped off the pavement.

If a human is like a cat, possessed of nine lives, I definitely cashed in one of my nine. My life could have ended, or I could have been severely injured. Had I had passengers with me, I would have been responsible for their severe injuries or deaths. This incident was a wake up call that I, an excellent driver, am not immune to an accident.

I vow I will never again put myself in such a position.

THE MILITARY

These are my thoughts on the military, based on my service in the US Army from 1952 to 1954. While the military services are much different today I believe these insights remain valid.

The Army (and the military) is a hugely dysfunctional bureaucracy.

It wastes huge amounts of money and resources and misuses its personnel.

The intelligence of soldiers is below average, and that of officers is average.

To succeed in the military one must learn to "play the game," "be social," have wives that advance a career, be conservative, not take chances, and follow orders.

When an intelligent officer finally becomes a command officer he has been so indoctrinated, he can rarely be an effective leader. This statement too often applies to those of General rank.

The military industrial complex is infinitely more powerful and fearful today than when President/General Dwight Eisenhower warned of its dangers in 1960.

In spite of the negatives, my military experience was, overall, a positive, which I am glad to have had.

SUMMER THUNDER

You said you were coming, warning us from the distant west.
We hear you roaring, louder and closer, stronger and nearer.
We hurry to sit on the porch where we hide from lightning
And cover our ears from the claps.

Moving fast you did but we wait for you to unleash your fury.

Ah . . . yes . . . there . . . fury . . .
The trees thank you for bending their trunks and exercising
their limbs.
The leaves thank you for their many drinks of water
And the trod upon grass raises its arms upward to the sky.

The big brown rock with the pink stripe is
Lighter now, washed of its uninvited dust.

And I thrill in the buffeting wind and driving rain,
as I stay dry on my protected porch.

You were always happy to be a drop-in who gives only
a moment's notice but won't stay for anything more than a
glancing blow
Never to accept our invitation to dinner or even a warm glass of
whiskey.
Sorry, I got more stops in the east and I must move on, you say.

And so you go on shaking the earth
Taking with you your thunder and lightning,

Your energy and majesty
Leaving us to sit on the porch
Reading the mail the postman brought.

He with the drip-dry shirt that is already dry
And he with the mail that has been protected
From the big drops of rain that used to
Spot letters when they were written in ink.

So I sit here with my whisky and my mail
Wishing you or your cousin come back
To thunder us
And bend our trunks
And shake our limbs
And wash our rocks
And love us.

MYTHS

When I saw that my slightly rotund Papa could not possibly slide down our tiny chimney, it was confirmed that Papa was not Santa Claus and that Santa was a hoax. I first gathered that this may be the case when we waited a whole hour for Santa to appear at the depot, and all he had for the several dozen boys who gathered was a piece of candy tossed into the crowd. Since other boys were standing nearer to the candy I didn't get any. How could there be a Santa when he was not fair in his gift giving?

I had already decided that the Easter Bunny was a myth, even before I knew the word "myth." Of course, that didn't keep me from hunting for as many eggs as I could find. Boiled eggs are smooth to hold in your hand and when they are colored they are appealing. And too, eating a hard-boiled egg was pleasant, if there was a handy saltshaker.

It bothered me that Santa was somehow going to visit all the houses in our Williamson town and our Mingo county—in the same night. Okay, maybe he could to that, but there are other towns in West Virginia. I have been to Huntington and I know that it is a big city with lots of houses.

There were just too many unanswered questions: Where does Santa park the sled and his reindeer when he goes down the chimney? Does Santa really go down the chimney? How does he keep his red suit free of soot? How do reindeer fly without wings? Really now, do they really fly? Why doesn't Santa run out of gifts before he leaves our street? The sled isn't that big! Please tell me so I can believe.

Ok, so there is no Easter Bunny and there is no Santa Claus and there are probably a lot of other things those big people told us that were not true.

AT THIRTY-FIVE

This short essay was written March 23, 1948 as an assignment in my high school senior English class, taught by our beloved Vera K. Randal. She always assigned two grades to our work: one for content and one for grammar. This is the only assignment that earned me an A for each. When Vera made a positive comment, she always found a way to balance the praise. "Sabet, your introduction is very clever [but] is all this theme your own?"

According to the fifth chapter of Genesis, Adam lived a total of 930 years, Methuselah lived 969 years, Mahalaleel lived 895 years and (poor old) Enoch lived only 365 years. I wonder what they were doing at the youthful age of thirty-five? Maybe they were recuperating from adolescence?

At thirty-five Thomas Edison was busy inventing the incandescent lamp, and William Shakespeare was writing his masterpiece, Hamlet. Theodore Roosevelt at thirty-five was being defeated for the mayoralty of New York City, and Jose Echegaray was fighting in the Spanish Revolution.

But enough I say, for the names of distant time. Let us consider the thoughts of one individual who will be in the short time of fifteen days one-half the age of thirty-five. For the sake of brevity we shall call this somnolent languor, I.

Now the question: what kind of man to I want to be at the age of thirty-five? The answer: frankly, I am not sure if I know. Of course, there are things that every boy in the country wants such as a good job, a wife, a home, and children.

I do know that I don't care to be a biblical character (as if I could), and I don't want to live 900 years. I don't want to be a famous inventor, writer or dramatist. But I do want to lead a simple, satisfying life, sprinkled with the essence of benevolence.

I once heard a preacher condemn the nine-out-of-ten men who "just want to be happy." But isn't that a goal highly desirable to attain? To say "my goal is to be happy" may sound a little selfish, and possibly it is; but consider the wonderful factors that constitute happiness, and those factors that are necessary for attainment—and think still of the prodigious by-products of that state of mind.

VII | TRAVELS WITH ABE

BASSETT TOURS, INC.
1986-2007

Lond003on was the destination in 1980 where I spent four weeks of my first sabbatical. Going to the theatre ten or more times a week was a sensible and highly justifiable activity for a theatre professor. It was a learning experience that I wish I could have experienced when I was an undergraduate. My boss, Liberal Arts Dean Eugene Cantelupe, allowed me to take another three weeks of sabbatical in 1982. This time I returned with Sharon and we spent most of our time going to the theatre, but added in a few out-of-town trips, mostly on Sundays. We both loved going to the theatre and we both loved England and dreamed about returning.

That is why in 1986 I began offering tours to London. The tours occurred during spring break at the University. Arrangements were made with a local travel agent to collect funds and pay invoices, thereby forgoing the university bureaucracy that would otherwise have resulted.

As I had been a co-founder of the Ohio Theatre Alliance, I had friends throughout Ohio who had already led London Theatre Tours. Each of them was extremely generous in sharing their knowledge. Although the reader will not know these persons, I recognize them here with deep gratitude: Bill Allman, Baldwin-Wallace College; Jake Rufli, Lakeview College; and Niels Riess, Ohio Northern University.

The first tour required a minimum of 15 persons to break even, and that number was reached only a few days before the registration deadline. The price of the tour was kept very low in an attempt to attract University personnel—faculty or students. Instead, I attracted theatregoers who tend to be highly educated and well to do. A winning formula was discovered; the London Theatre Tour ended with a 20-year history. Many of our clients became our friends as they repeated their annual March trip to London. Some traveled with us 16 of the 20 tours. In 2000 we had a group of 40 persons with half joining us for an add-on tour to Spain. While this was an exceptionally large travel group, most were repeat clients who were able to function on their own with no hand-holding by the two tour leaders.

There were several memorable occurrences on that first trip to London. We were booked into an inexpensive Bed and Breakfast hotel with very small rooms. It was truly wall-to-wall bedding with hardly enough room to turn in. And yet, no one complained. Second, my booking agent was to have bought tickets for a Shakespearean production at Stratford-on-Avon. However, no play was scheduled for our date, but as she had booked a coach and driver, she suggested we visit Shakespeare's home in Stratford-Upon-Avon. Our coach was small, slow, and underpowered, making us late in returning home. On our way through Oxford, our hungry travelers asked to stop to eat. Not having directions, we hailed an Oxford student who led us to an ancient but popular student lair, which would never have been found except for his guidance. We were hungry so the food was tasty and the unique ambience made for a great adventure.

This was a true, old pub with a low ceiling blackened by years of fires in the wide fireplace. We sat scattered around the dark little room on genuine antique stools, tables and sofas, amidst the students and locals. Was it upscale? Hardly! But the atmosphere was emphatically genuine.

Two of the people on that first tour—one married, one estranged, returned on the third tour as a married couple. They traveled with us for the next 15 years.

Each year our London Tour was upgraded to slightly better

hotels, and more amenities were added. The activities began with a city bus tour, and there were guided walks often led by actors, sometimes singing actors. We walked The Inns of Court, Dickens' London, Sherlock Holmes and 221B Baker Street, Famous Pubs, and various areas of the city. The Portobello Flea Market was an optional but popular place to visit. We took in visits to London's entire major art institutions and many minor galleries; we arranged meetings with actors, critics, and theatre managers. Building on that first impromptu trip to Strafford-upon-Avon, we scheduled day trips to attractions within a day's drive of London. These visits took us to the Cotswolds, Brighton, Dover, Winchester, Hampshire, East Anglia, and to many stately homes. We visited Churchill's birthplace, Blenheim Palace in Oxfordshire, and his family home in later life, Chartwell in Kent. One year we took the train to Yorkshire, which was a good long trip.

The London Theatre Tour had in fact become a Theatre and Art tour. Our son Douglas and his wife Paola and her parents joined us on three occasions. Luigi Penzo (Gigi) did not speak English fluently, but he had an encyclopedic knowledge of the fine arts. Once at an exhibit of the paintings of Caravaggio at the National Gallery, Gigi commented on the history of each painting while his wife Iva translated.

On six occasions, I offered successful add-on tours. Three times we went to Paris, and once each to Ireland, Belgium and Holland, and Spain. In all the years that Douglas lived in Italy he came to London to visit us and see the plays. He came to know all the regulars who came with us virtually every year. One year we were leaving the hotel on the way to the airport when Douglas cried out that we were missing a couple. Indeed, we had left them at the hotel. We returned to the hotel to fetch them, with great relief for all, especially the couple left behind.

In the beginning, in 1986, it was necessary to have a London agent book hotel, transportation and plays. With experience I was able to do my own booking, aided by the spreading use of the fax machine, the lowering cost of overseas telephoning, and of course, in time, the Internet. At first one had to depend on a library's copy of the London *Times* to know what plays were offered and their quality. With the Internet, one could scan the newspaper reviews shortly after a play opened.

I have kept my booklet programs from all these years. It is a remarkable history of our activities. (What shall I do with this collection?) The reader may ask if these tours were profitable. Yes, of course, but they were most profitable in the opportunity Sharon and I was afforded to travel and to become culturally enriched. Our first flights were on British Air and they offered us free transportation, sometimes in Business Class, for "scouting trips."

Why were we successful in this venture? There were several reasons: the tours were reasonably priced, below the cost of comparable tours; it was seen as a good value. People were also attracted to our tours because the tour operator was the tour leader and a professional theatre person who led discussions after the play. Sharon and I were the responsible people who had a vested interest in the success of the tour and we were there to solve any problem that might arise.

And, importantly, there was the element of friendship. Greeting our travelers each year was greeting good friends.

To this day, we miss seeing them.

. . . . .

When I left Wright State University in 1988 to become Dean of the School of Fine and Performing Arts at Indiana University Purdue University Fort Wayne, I continued touring, with profits going to my new University. My mailing listed expanded greatly, with many people from Indiana joining those from Ohio. The tour grew by word of mouth. A traveler who became a good friend was David Moore, former Dean of the College of

Business at Cornell University. One year I had eight people from his hometown of Ponte Verde, Florida, all friends of David. I asked if he had solicited people to come on the tour and he said no, he merely told people when they asked where he had been and they said they would like to go too.

In 1994, when I retired from Indiana and returned to Ohio, I decided to keep the tour going as a privately owned company. I incorporated as Bassett Tours, Inc. and became licensed by the Secretary of State as a Tour Operator. My company became bonded and I was insured. It was in this year that I developed a new tour to the Middle East.

In 1992, I had visited Damascus where a nephew was a Fulbright Scholar. I managed to enter Lebanon, visiting the mountain village of my parents' birth as well as Beirut. The civil war was mostly finished but the US Department of State strongly discouraged Americans from visiting Lebanon.

Returning to Damascus from Lebanon, my nephew and I traveled to southeast Syria and the quaint small town of Deir Ezzor on the Euphrates River. I was overcome with awe and wonderment as I beheld that storied river where civilization began nearly 10,000 years earlier. We also stopped in the ancient town of Palmyra, where majestic ruins tell of the great history of Syria. The Syrians like to say that if you have never studied Syria's history you have never studied Western Civilization.

It was then that I made plans for a two-week tour to Jordan and Syria with a single day in Lebanon. We had tours in 1995, 1996 and 1998. In Jordan, Amman, Petra, Madaba and the Red Sea were major attractions. In Syria, Damascus and Aleppo were the major cities while Hama, Latakia and Deir Ezor were smaller but very interesting cities. We visited major archaeological sites throughout both countries.

In 1998, at the end of the two weeks in Jordan and Syria my family group spent another week in Lebanon. They

were our son Douglas, my sisters Selma and Lorraine, and
two nieces (Nancy Griffith and Jan Rutherdale). We had a
Lebanese guide and a large van with a driver. We visited all
the major cities including Beirut, Tyre, Sour, and Tripoli. The
visit to Baalbek, home to one of the world's best-preserved
Roman ruins, was incredible as was our visit to the Cedars
of Lebanon. We visited our parents' ancestral home, Kfeir
Zeit, situated at 2500 feet above sea level on the slopes of Mt.
Hermon. We also made contact with members of the Bassett
family in Kab Elias in the Baaka Valley.

In Lebanon's Bekaa valley, at Kab Elias, my touring family met with two related
Bassett Families.

VISITING LEBANON

The basis of this article is a letter written to Helena LaHood,
a Lebanese friend living in New Zealand.

One of my goals is to make sense of the genealogy information I gathered over the years. Our history is very sketchy, and there is little documentation to back up what we know or what we think we know. I was told by a village elder, now deceased, that my mother's family, the Saad family, moved to Kfeir Zeit from the Ras Matn region, which is in the mountains just to the east of Beirut. They moved in the 1700s. My mother's father, Assef Saad, was the village butcher, and my mother, as a young girl, assisted him by collecting payment from the buyers.

Apparently my father's family was in the village even longer, but there is no written documentation. Before my father immigrated to America at age 16, he trained as a cobbler, presumably with his father. Through marriage, we are related on my father's side to the Abourezks, the Hannas, the Kawajas, the Tweels, the Cantees, and many more families. In fact, on both sides of the family we are related to virtually every family in the village.

Fortunately, a first cousin, Victor Bassett, became interested in his genealogy in the late 1940s and started questioning his father and his father's contemporaries. He was able to gather a great deal of information that probably takes us back to the early 1900s. We will not get further back because church records were destroyed in the Druze-Christian conflicts of 1840 and 1860.

My first visit to Kfeir in 1992 was emotional and spiritual. I insisted on walking the last mile into the town. Kfeir is at an altitude of 2500 feet above sea level and the air is clean, cool and sweet. I walked the road through groves of olive trees. I felt the spirit of my parents. I felt I was there on their behalf, and they had awoken from their slumber to share the moment with me.

Each person I saw recognized immediately that I was foreign to the village. "Who are you?" What is your name?" Who are you coming to see?" My name, I would say in broken Arabic— "Ibrahim al-Bassiet, my father is from the house of al-Bassiet, and my mother is from the house of Saad."

"Welcome to your village," they said in greeting. Everyone would invite me into their house or store, including the Druze, who now comprise 60% of the population. They offered me tea and coffee and soft drinks. If I had accepted everything offered, it would have taken a week to move through the small village.

My mother's house is occupied by a descendent of the Saad family. My father's house on the lower street of the village is now derelict with no floors or roof to go with the still standing stonewalls.

Visiting the village was especially exciting, since in 1992, I was virtually the first foreigner who had come to visit the ancestral grounds since the outbreak of the civil war in April 1975. The Department of State was disallowing travel by US citizens. I had to sneak into Lebanon from Syria with good luck and the help of a Syrian family I contacted in Damascus.

Retiring as a university professor in 1994, I incorporated myself as a tour promoter. Three times I led tours to the Middle East, mainly Jordan and Syria with one day in Lebanon. I came to understand and love those countries. I say to people that you cannot fully appreciate Lebanon unless you spend time in Syria first. The history of Syria and Jordan is the history of Western Civilization and it leads to understanding their culture. Lebanon was part of the Ottoman Empire for 400 years, and also a part of the province of Syria. The history of Lebanon and Syria are intertwined to this day. A Lebanese friend who lives nearby told me I could not be a Lebanese, because I was too tall; I must be a Syrian.

The moment one crosses over the border into Lebanon you sense that you are in a different country. It starts with the way people walk; they are jauntier, and there is a touch more swagger. There is more free enterprise. Lebanese are different from Syrians.

Our tour guide in Lebanon often talked about "the Arabs" coming into Lebanon. She was referring to the Muslims who came from the Arabian Peninsula after 650 A.D. I asked her if she was an Arab. "No." she blurted back, "I am Phoenician."

The interesting thing about that assertion is that it is a political statement made by a Lebanese Maronite Christian that she is not an Arab and not a Muslim.

I have learned that there are two definitions of who is an Arab: a person whose native language is Arabic or a person whose native country is a member of the 22-nation Arab League. When touring the National Museum in Beirut we made an interesting discovery. On display were small rectangular stones bearing messages and statements about the deceased. One inscription was particularly touching saying, "Dear Antigone, we loved you so much, you were too young to die, we shall always miss you." The stone, from about the time of Christ, was written in Greek, one of the important languages of the times.

We descendants of Lebanon have always wondered about our origins. When I had my DNA analyzed by the National Geographic, I made a startling discovery about how long my ancestors have been in the Lebanon area. I am a homo sapiens like all men upon the earth. We have a common father, an "Adam," if you will. Our "Adam" lived 50 or 60 thousand years ago in East Africa. Over the centuries, the tribes began a slow northerly movement, following the herds that sought new areas for grazing. The northern movement stopped when the tribes learned how to plant seeds and harvest crops. They transformed themselves from hunter-gathers into agriculturalists. This occurred about 8,000 B.C., and is marked as the beginning of modern civilization, when people began organizing themselves into communities. My DNA tribe settled in the northern Fertile Crescent, which includes Lebanon, Palestine and the west coast of Syria. The Baaka Valley of Lebanon, situated between two mountain ranges, is an incredibly fertile place where seeds can flourish and people with them.

This scientific analysis tells me that my distant ancestors have lived in the area of Lebanon for ten thousand years! We predated the Phoenicians!

PEDDLERS ARE ENTREPRENEURS

Papa's world of work in America began as a peddler. That many Lebanese immigrants to America in the early 20th century began their work as peddlers is quite logical, for in the old country, craftsmen and merchants would sometimes walk to neighboring villages to offer their wares.

In America, they used homemade wooden boxes strapped to their backs, filled with merchandise, offering goods to those who lived on farms, where most of America's population resided at the turn of the century. This system allowed the immigrants to learn English and American ways, and it also permitted them to accumulate financial resources, which were used for important priorities. First in importance was to buy passage for those left behind, including wives and mothers, and brothers and sisters. The second objective was to be able to purchase a farm, or to establish a business. A peddler worked for himself and required very little capital to start a business and capital accumulation was easier in the days before income taxes and business fees.

Papa and his father arrived in America in 1901. Five years passed before the remaining members of the family could immigrate in 1906. By this time, Joseph and Abraham had acquired or were renting a farmhouse with several acres of farmland. By 1910, Joseph was the owner of this land. People from the mountains of Lebanon would not have known much about Midwest farming, but they knew about hard work and became successful farmers.

In time my father Abraham moved beyond peddling into storefront businesses. He first affiliated himself with his brother-in-law, Moses Bassett, in Madison, West Virginia (1914) in the grocery business. He then partnered with another brother-in-law, Sam Saad, in the same business in Pikeville, Kentucky (1915). By the time of the 1920 census he was the manager/owner of a "fruit stand" in Williamson, West Virginia. A photograph of this store shows that he sold many items beyond fruits: ice cream, canned food, sodas, etc. He quickly learned to sell whatever it was that customers wanted to buy. In time, his "fruit stand" became a confectionary store where he made and sold fudge and other sweet candies. At Christmas time, his store was stocked with tables filled with homemade fudge and hard rock candy purchased from vendors. Much of the candy may have come from Toledo, Ohio, where a cousin, Sam Bassett, owned a candy factory. Bassett's Confectionary store also sold newspapers, sandwiches, sodas, and ice cream. In time, beer and sandwiches were added as well as a jukebox and a pinball machine.

Hard work was the norm for my father. He opened his confectionary store in the morning and locked the door at night. A few times I was with him late at night waiting for him to finish mopping the linoleum floor. He did every job he had to do to run a business that earned his family's subsistence.

As a successful businessman, he knew he must constantly reinvest into the business. On Sunday mornings a rush of customers came to buy copies of *The Cincinnati Enquirer* that arrived on a southbound Norfolk & Western passenger train, and *The Times* of Roanoke, Virginia, that arrived on northbound train. It was fortuitous that the confectionary store was directly across the street from the train station.

The store's income during the depression was augmented after my father purchased and installed slot machines. They were placed in the "back room" of the store and also in several other locations throughout the county. I have no specific knowledge of how this illegal activity was arranged, but there is no question, knowing small town politics in West Virginia, that Papa "paid off" the Sheriff. My Dad was a 32nd degree Mason, as were many of the town's businessmen, and the contacts one made in this charitable and influential organization were always important and useful.

Lebanese immigrants loved their new country and quickly adapted. They believed in the adage that America was "the great melting pot." They worked to become productive and loyal citizens of America, grateful for the opportunities that were presented to them.

MY FATHER'S FAMILY

The photograph of the family of Joseph and Miriam Bassett was taken in 1918 at the time that Frank was to be sent overseas to join the American Expeditionary Force in France. From left to right are Hicebee, Sleiman (Sam), Ferris (Frank) and Ibrihim (Abraham). Seated are Yousef (Joseph) and Miriam (Mary).

Joseph Bassett (Yousef al-Bassiet)
1843-1926

My grandfather, Joseph Bassett, was born in 1843 in the mountain village of Kfeir Zeit, in what is now Lebanon, but at the time was part of the Ottoman Empire in the province of Syria. At the time of his immigration to America in 1901, those from Lebanon were often labeled as being nationals of Syria or Turkey. Only occasionally were they marked as immigrants of Lebanon.

In his naturalization papers of January 2, 1906 he renounced all allegiance to the Sultan of Turkey (as if there were any at all.) Renunciation was not difficult to do as

Lebanon, at the turn of the century, was under the domination of the Ottoman Empire and had been so for nearly 400 years. As immigrants to America, they did not turn their backs, however, on their native food or dance or allegiance to family, and many continued to read papers in their native language. But adapting to their adopted country was an important goal, as was being perceived as loyal Americans.

In spite of the fact that my grandfather Joseph died four years before I was born, I feel a strong kinship with him, in part because of the way he looks in the three photos I have of him, and the stories told about him.

Joseph, the son of Ferris Bassett and Regina Tweel, had one brother, Salim, and seven sisters, each of whom married into one of the Kfeirian families: Tweel, Cantees, Kawaja, Bolus, Michael, Thabet and Margi, making him an uncle to many, many nephews and nieces. In the village of Kfeir one could, with great certainty, call any other person "cousin." It was the long established custom to marry within the village, and when one married outside the village, it may have been marriage to one at least distantly related. The common notion that all people from this part of the world are brown-eyed is not true. My father had blue-green eyes, as did four of his six children.

The Bassett house in Kfeir, situated on the lowest level of the village, was sold to a member of the Tweel family with the proceeds financing the cost of immigration to America. Joseph was 58 years old when he came to America in 1901 with his sixteen-year-old eldest son, Abraham Joseph, my father. I have yet to locate his port of entry. Many Kfeirians had immigrated to the United States in 1895, and a few even earlier, but he waited until his eldest son was of a sufficiently mature age so they could travel and work together. As with many Kfeirians, they first came to Toledo, Ohio, where earlier Kfeirians had settled.

The 1910 census identifies Joseph as a farmer and Abraham as a peddler. Joseph's wife Miriam immigrated in 1906 together with their son Frank (Fares) and daughter Hicebee. Their son Sam (Salim) was apparently turned away at a US port of entry because of conjunctivitis, a contagious eye condition known as "pink eye," joining the family at a later date. Joseph settled on a farm about four miles north of Blissfield, Michigan in Lenawee County. The farm was in his grandson's hands as late as 2012, meaning the farm was in family hands for more than 110 years.

There are two stories about Joseph. My first cousin, Minnie Kerbawy, now deceased, recalled with pleasure Joseph's frequent Saturday visits to Blissfield. He came to town on a horse drawn cart to buy supplies and would stop by the Kerbawy house. He was jovial and always wore a smile, and Minnie and her younger sisters and brothers looked forward to seeing him.

When I was a child, my mother told me that when Joseph became sick and was near death, he was put on a diet that featured a great deal of laban (yogurt) and that in time he regained his health, living a few more years.

Mariam (Mary) Jamra Bassett
1863–1957

Joseph's wife, Mariam or Mary (1863-1957), came to America in 1906 at the age of 43, but unlike her husband or children, she did not speak or read English. My father Abraham was very devoted to his mother, and the family often made the trip from our home in West Virginia to the farm in southern Michigan. Papa always brought his mother a bottle of whiskey among other gifts. We young children

 were required to enter the house to see our grandmother as the first order of business. She would, on seeing us, starting talking a mile a minute in Arabic, giving us kisses on one cheek and then the other, only to repeat it again and again. My youngest sister and I, who knew very little Arabic, could never understand what she was saying. Even if we had known Arabic,

she talked so quickly, we wouldn't have understood. But we knew she was delighted to see us. After a sufficient time had elapsed—only a few minutes—we were given permission to leave the room and to go outside to play.

Grandmother Mariam was a diminutive person, about five feet tall. She had a lovely face, even as an older person with a wrinkled face. She passed away in 1957 at the age of 94. She and Joseph are buried in the Pleasant View Cemetery in Blissfield, Michigan.

Abraham Joseph Bassett
1885-1949

I was only 18 years old when my father died, too young to learn of his history. Papa never talked to me about himself or his past. As his entire family, and most of his cousins lived in America, he considered himself an American. It was assumed that any remaining relative in Lebanon would eventually come to America.

While many of his generation may have been reluctant to talk about their heritage or to exhibit sentimentalism about their village of origin or their country, they certainly embraced their heritage in terms of food, dance, celebrations and loyalty to their larger family.

The thirteen years between his arrival in America in 1901 and 1914 when he and my mother were married is without verifiable history except that the 1910 census identified him as a peddler. It is probable that he helped his father accumulate the cash to buy the farm and was a part owner. Nothing in his demeanor or speech ever suggested to me that he worked as a farmer, but it is possible he did help on the farm.

After his marriage to Rahija Saad in Blissfield, Michigan, the newlyweds settled in Madison, West Virginia, where Abraham's sister Hicebee and her husband Moses lived. The oldest daughter, Gladys Shumla, was born in Madison in 1915, but Selma was born in Pikeville, Kentucky in 1916, and Wadad in Williamson, West Virginia in 1917. The 1920 census shows Abraham is the "owner and manager" of a "cigar and fruit stand."

Gladys, the eldest daughter, wrote about her father: "Papa loved having people around. We had company on holidays and special occasions, but his most fun time is when he was at a party in a large hall. Papa had the greatest smile. He was so cute dancing around and smiling that great smile of his. People really enjoyed his good times."

Selma recalls Papa as the lead dancer of the dubke, vigorously swinging a handkerchief in his free hand, as was the custom. The dubke is a traditional, circular line dance with a set dance step, but one that invites variations. The dance is done to a very strong drumbeat and is a highlight of the annual Kfeirian Reunion.

Papa was one of the group of men who helped create an annual meeting of the descendants of the village of Kfeir. This became known as the Kfeirian Reunion and is still being held 80 years after its founding. The second annual reunion was held in Williamson in 1933 at the Masonic Lodge. Papa was a 32nd degree Mason. I was a small child but I have memories of being in the Lodge. It was my only visit.

Only a few yards from the Lodge, on the corner of Logan Street and Fourth Avenue, was Bassett's Confectionary store. Through the years, Papa reinvested in his business, carrying goods the public wished to buy. At Christmas, the store was full of hard rock candy and homemade fudge. The store was the central place to purchase Sunday newspapers, which were delivered to the Norfolk & Western depot directly across the street. The first, contemporary, low-seat soda counter was installed in the late thirties, and sandwiches and beer were sold. Papa was a true entrepreneur.

The owners of the building that housed the Confectionary decided to sell the building. If Papa had been successful in his bid to purchase the building, he would have stayed in Williamson. In 1946, he bought the Towne Tavern in Columbus and the family settled in a splendid house in the suburb of Upper Arlington.

The new house at 2015 Tremont Road was three stories with basement. There were four bedrooms on the second floor, and a finished bedroom on the third floor, formerly an attic. A coal-burning furnace that is labor-intensive, as coal must be shoveled into the furnace at regular intervals heated the house. After a winter of dealing with the situation, an automatic conveyer belt was installed.

All new furniture was purchased at Lazarus Department Store in downtown Columbus. This included a handsome dining room, which was later damaged by fire in Selma's house. I had the set refinished to its original state and it is now in my house.

The Towne Tavern, across the street from the YWCA and the Union Department Store on Long Street in downtown Columbus was packed nightly with servicemen during 1945. After the war when the soldiers and sailors returned to civilian life, and television became a popular mode of entertainment, tavern business subsided.

Sam (Sleiman) Bassett
1887- 1955

Uncle Sam was a favorite uncle for his wry sense of humor and for his kindnesses. My cousin Victor Bassett and I think that when Sam came to America he was denied entry, possibly because of "pink eye," which was a contagious condition. According to Uncle Frank, Sam had a sty on his eye, a condition due to malnutrition. Having been rejected, he found his way to a seaport where he became a merchant seaman for one or two years.

Uncle Sam's stories were related to the sea: stories of foreign ports and drunken brawls. He once claimed to have lost a pocket watch over the railing of a ship, which he later recovered in the belly of a fish purchased on shore. Even as young children we were dubious of such wild and fantastic stories, but Uncle Sam never backed down. He also told of visits to foreign ports and far off countries. There is little doubt that Sam had experience as a merchant seaman. A young, strong, healthy immigrant easily qualified as an "able bodied seaman" since physical strength was a far more important requirement than verbal or language skills or formal education.

When he arrived in America, sometime between 1906 and 1910, he came as an illegal immigrant according to a story told by Uncle Frank. "Because Abraham and I feared that he would be rejected because of his eye problem, we went to Windsor (Ontario) in the winter, and brought him across the frozen Detroit River." While this is an interesting story, it is just as likely that Uncle Sam crossed the Detroit River in a boat-taxi.

Uncle Sam settled on the farm, spending the rest of his

life as a farmer. After the death of Grandfather Joseph in 1926, my Papa offered to "sign over" the farm to Sam, with the provision that Sam stay on the farm to take care of their mother.

Uncle Sam married Farha (Flora) Abourezk (1900–1983) who came to America in 1920, living initially in Winner, South Dakota; she came to Toledo, Ohio, to work at the Corey Candy Company. She and Sam were married in 1928 when Sam was 40 and Farha 30. This was an arranged marriage, as were many marriages of the day. Farha was an animated, energetic, take charge woman, and Uncle Sam, the world traveler, hemmed in between a bossy wife and the obligation to take care of his mother, was not happy in his marriage.

Uncle Sam and Aunt Farha had two children, both boys. Joseph Samuel, named after his grandfather and father, became a heart surgeon. He worked his way through undergraduate and medical school, all on his own. A second son, Alexander, a special needs person was institutionalized, passing away in 1951 at the age of 18.

In 1945 or 1946, a locomotive struck Uncle Sam's car as he was crossing train tracks, causing severe injuries. A life long smoker of cigarettes, he died of cancer in 1955. Aunt Farha suffered from Alzheimer's disease in her later years. On my last visit to see her on the farm she vehemently insisted that the telephone wires be cut. I disconnected the wires without causing permanent damage.

Hicebee Bassett
1892-1974

Hicebee Bassett was the third of the four children, the most diminutive, but taller than her mother. She immigrated to America in 1906. At 17 years of age, she married a second or third cousin, 30-year old Moses Bassett, January 10, 1910. Hicebee and Moses had an arranged marriage, marrying in the Greek Orthodox Church in Toledo. They had three sons. Edward was born in 1911 in Toledo, Dewey in 1914 in Madison, West Virginia, and Victor in 1920 in Welch, West Virginia.

Aunt Hicebee and Uncle Moses, after first living in Toledo, Ohio moved to Madison, West Virginia, but by 1922 had settled in Napoleon, Ohio where they owned and operated a five-and-dime store. Every Christmas we received a large box of gifts for the entire family: handkerchiefs, linens, socks, and other items from the store.

Hicebee and Moses lived all their lives in the same brick two-story house on a quiet street in Napoleon. Edward worked with his father, eventually owning the five-and-dime. Dewey and Victor both graduated from Ohio State University, one in Electrical Engineering and the other in Psychology. The three sons produced two grandchildren: Edward's David and Dewey's Deborah.

Aunt Hicebee was a quiet-spoken and loving woman who was always happy to see me. As a child, I loved visiting them in Napoleon because their brick house was on a fine street, the city was clean and neat, and the nearby Maumee River was grand.

In 1907, Hicebee flanked by brothers Abraham and Samuel

In her late years, Hicebee had heart problems and was operated on by her nephew Dr. Joseph Bassett, who implanted a pacemaker. Her last years were spent in a Napoleon nursing home, where I visited one time. She seemed so sad, perhaps, waiting for death.

Frank (Ferris) Bassett
1896-1990

Uncle Frank seemed to be an urbane sophisticate who adapted to American ways more than any in his family, at least to judge by his dapper way of dressing. Where Abe was a businessman always with vest and suit, and Uncle Sam was a farmer whose bib overalls never closeted with a suit, Frank wore sport coats and fedora hats.

All the brothers spoke with an accent, but Frank's accent had the least Arabic influence, having entered the United States at a younger age (11) than his brothers. Frank, being the last to be married, was freer to travel and to associate with non-immigrants.

No doubt his service in the United States Army brought him into contact with common Americans. It was in the service that he learned to cook, which led him into his chief occupation in life, that of a restaurateur.

Uncle Frank was proud of his military service and particularly of his role during World War I in Europe with the American Expeditionary Force in France. It was after his death that we learned that he arrived in France on November 11, 1918, the day the armistice was signed

Frank was married and divorced, sometime in the 1920s, to a Pauline Hagan. This bit of history was never talked about and no other information is available. Later in life he married Jean (Eugenia) Karpinsky, the daughter of Polish immigrants, who earned her living as a hairdresser. They were a splendid match, each adoring the other. Both were childless. Aunt Jean was a lovely woman.

On the occasion of Frank's 80th birthday, my cousin Joseph Bassett and I sponsored a birthday party in Detroit, with nearly 50 friends and family in attendance.

Jean passed away in 1989 and Frank seemed never to recover from his loss. At one point he said he didn't understand why God allowed him to continue living without Jean. He stayed in their house in Detroit for a year. His nephew Dewey Bassett, my first cousin, assumed responsibility of caring for Frank, traveling from Dayton to Detroit every two months. When Frank's health deteriorated, Dewey brought Frank to a nursing home in Kettering, Ohio. It was here that Frank passed away in 1990 at the age of 94.

THE BASSETT GENEALOGY

The genealogy of the Bassett (al-Bassiet) family cannot be traced with certainty beyond the 19th century because church records were destroyed in the 1840 and 1860 Druze-Christian uprisings. I am thankful to have learned that my great-grandfather, Farris Bassett, who married Regina Tweel, had two sons and seven daughters. This information has been recorded in a Family Tree Maker genealogy chart that I have maintained.

The value and accuracy of the oral tradition of record keeping cannot be discounted. When I first went to Kfeir, Lebanon, in 1992, I met the village elder Aref al-Khoury, whose sister Najla married Eli Bassett of Welch, West Virginia. Aref lived with them for a few years in the 1920s. He attended high school there, developing excellent English speaking and writing skills. We exchanged several letters in the next few years, before he passed away.

Our family lore identifies our clan as "Kaboosh" which we were told meant "curly haired." Asking Aref if the name "Kaboosh" was used to distinguish our clan, he replied in the negative. Kaboosh is not a family name; "it is either a nickname or a proper noun and has nothing to do with the genealogy of the Bassetts." In the Arab world, he explained, the nickname sometimes supplants the original family name through frequent usage. For example, the name Kasir was the word for short; Taweel or Tweel was tall; and Asmar was brown.

A question often asked is how did our family come by the name Bassett. That is a legitimate query as "Bassett" is a common English name. The name also exists in France as "Basset" with one 't' and pronounced bah-SAY, and in Italy as "Bassetti", pronounced bahs-SET-tee. None of these variations is in any way related to the Arabic name, which is pronounced al-buh-SEET. [Some have asked if the name could have been adopted during the Crusades, but this is unlikely. It is also unlikely that the Crusaders dropped their "seeds" to give the fair skin and light colored eyes found in the Middle East.]

Converting the Arabic alphabet into the English alphabet has always been difficult to do. The best rule is to spell in English the way the name sounds in Arabic. Thus al-buh-SEET becomes, at first, Bassiet. The "al" in Arabic is the definite article 'the' and is not usually translated into names in English.

When I made my first visit to our village in Lebanon, I drew snickers when I said my name was "bah-SEET." Without the "al," bah-SEET means simple, as in simple-minded. My first cousin Ernest McCarus, the renowned Arabic scholar, speculates, "there may have been a man who was 'simple, straightforward and uncomplicated' receiving the sobriquet 'the direct and honest one' al-baSiit; his family then were related to al-baSiit, which became the family name."

As mentioned elsewhere in this volume, Grandfather Joseph's name was first recorded as "al-Bassiet" on his naturalization papers of 1906, but by the time of the 1910 census, the name was spelled Bassett and was probably pronounced in the English way by native speakers. No doubt the Bassett cousins conferred among themselves to standardize the spelling.

However, having said that, variations remain. The Bassetts of St. Albans, West Virginia (our cousins) went with Bassitt; and my own Uncle Frank chose Bassiet even though he used the English pronunciation. With the accent falling on the first syllable in Bassett, the ending of "ett," "itt," or "it" will render the same pronunciation.

In response to my question about the origins of the Bassett family, Araf confirms that the Bassett family history in Kfeir and Kab-Elias were destroyed during the troubles of 1840 between the Druze and Christians. He said the late Abdullah Bassett of Kfeir tried to collect as much information as possible about the history of his family from his father and uncles. He was around eighty years old when he wrote the following:

> "From Kissirwan in northern Lebanon, the Bassetts came to Kfeir some three or four hundred years ago [1500 to 1600 a.d.] beginning their lives as weavers, farmers, and merchants. Then, from Kfeir, they spread out to Kab-Elias in the Bakaa; Rashaya el-Foukhar in the District of Hasbaya; Damascus; Houran in Syria; and Kafir Yasif in Palestine. They also went to the Mountain of the Druze [Malah, Jabel Druze] in south-eastern Syria, and also to Egypt."

Aref, continuing with his narrative, recalls what he knows of the Bassett family:
"Some members of this family were outstanding men in their days.

- Dr. Sabir Bassett graduated from the American University of Beirut and spent all his life in Cairo, Egypt, where he also died.
- Tanel, son of Abou Mulhim Bassett, was a famous musician who played the oud and served as an officer in the Turkish army. He passed away at the house of his friend Amir Fakour, Chief of the Fadil tribes in the Houran area of southwestern Syria.
- Among these famous men were also Abou Mulhim and Abdullah, who were the oldest men in the family.

Abdullah was very fond of reading history and was happy to relate historical events. He was one of the few Christian men who escaped assassinations at Hasbaya during the bloody massacres of the Christians in this area in 1860.

- Nicola Bassett went to the U.S.A., returned here, and also had boys who went to America; some died here (in Kfeir) and others there.

- The living that are known to the author are Philip Bassett of Huntington, West Virginia, and his cousin Solomon Bassett of Toledo, Ohio. Information about their cousins in the U.S.A. is not known by the author of this study.

- Nassif Abou Nassar Bassett became Kfeir's Mukhtar [mayor] for a good number of years, and his son, the late Mikhail, was the telephone operator and the municipal secretarial clerk.

- Nabih went to the U.S.A. and studied mechanical engineering in Toledo, Ohio. His brother Hafiz is a successful merchant there also.

- Jurius and his brother John [first or second cousin to my father Abraham] lived at St. Albans, West Virginia all their lives. Nassib, one of Jurius's boys, graduated from West Point Military Academy and served as an officer on the staff of General McArthur during the 2nd World War in the Pacific theater. His brothers, Adeeb and Nasseb, are merchants in West Virginia. They were born at St. Albans in the same state where their Uncle John also lived.

- Nassif Bassett, son of Mikhail, died in Charleston, West Virginia. His brother Soulieman went to Africa.

- During an Israeli raid on Kfeir, Kamal Bassett, son of Mikhail Kaboosh Bassett, had both hands cut off and now he is living without hands. Yet, the Palestinian commandos pay him a monthly salary. [I saw Kamal on my visit to Kfeir in 1992.]

• After selling their property in Kfeir to the Tweel family,
  Joseph Bassett [my grandfather] and his cousins migrated
  to the U.S.A. Their large houses were in the southern
  section of the town, overlooking the green valley below.
  They are now in ruins. Joseph's sons were Ibrahim, Salim,
  and Faris [Abraham, Sam & Frank] and they lived in
  West Virginia, Ohio, and Michigan.
• We know nothing about the members of the family who
  went to Palestine. Of those who went to Damascus,
  George and Issa, were tailors. Of those in Jabel Druze we
  know nothing. Nor do we know about those in Kab-Elias."

. . . . .

One interested in knowing the location of the place names cited
above will easily find them on an online map of Lebanon.

• Kab Elias is in the Bakaa Valley, east of Beirut and south
  of Zahle.
• Kisserwan is the general area of Lebanon immediately north
  of Beirut stretching from the Mediterranean to the Bakaa.
• Rachaiya is seven air miles north of Kfeir.
• The Jabel Druze is a high plateau area of 2500 feet above
  sea level in southern Syria. Members of the Bassiet family
  live in Malah, Jebel Druze, Syria. I visited in 1997.
• Kafir Yasif is in the Western Galilee area of northwest Israel.
• The Hauran is in the southwest portion of Syria and
  includes the cities of Daara and Busra.

. . . . .

In my travels in the Middle East, I have met several people who
were unknown to Aref. They include:

• Fred Bassett in Damascus. One of his daughters lives in
  Montreal and another in Florida.
• Nimer Bassett Markos and his family live in the Western
  Galilee section of Israel in the town of Kfir Yessif.

Sharon and I visited in 1997 and have maintained
contact with the family. They have three daughters,
one of whom is a professional singer and the other a
dancer. Nimer passed away in 2013 and was highly
esteemed throughout Palestine and the Arab portions
of Israel. He was mayor of Kfir Yessif and was a member
of the Communist Party, the only viable choice for an Arab
Christian in Israel.

- I traveled to the Jebel Druze area of southern Syria to the
town of Malah, where I met several Bassett families who
were descendants of three Bassett brothers who settled in
Syria about 1870.
- In Kab Elias in the Bakaa Valley, we met two Bassett
families. [See the photograph on page 176.]

MY MOTHER'S FAMILY
The Family of George Saad

My maternal great-great-grandfather is Khalil and Jamillie Saad according to the Kfeirian Ancestry web site. One of their children is George (Jurius) Saad, my maternal great-grandfather, who fathered three children: Assaf, Ayoub, and Helena. Assaf is the father of my mother.

Of the Saad family, Aref El-Khouri, an elder of the village of Kfeir, told me, during my visit of 1992, that the Saad family came to Kfeir in the 1700's from Ras el Matn, a mountainous community just east of Beirut. In Kfeir, the Saads were butchers.

The families of Assaf and Ayoub Saad in Kfeir, Lebanon in 1900. Assaf seated left center picture Ayoub seated right center, Rahija standing at right, Uncles Sam and Jasper standing at center, and Helena at right.

Assaf Saad
1859 – 1937

When I first visited Kfeir in 1992, I met an elder who told me he remembered my grandfather Assaf who was born February 2 or March 6, 1859, and died in the 1930s. His brother Ayoub was younger, born in 1872, and was a more handsome man. Assaf has the distinction of being among the first in the Saad family to come to America, arriving at Ellis Island on June 8, 1895. He was one of a contingent of about 40 persons from Kfeir who traveled together. The average age of the group was 23 years. Included in the group were his fourteen-year-old daughter Maheba, and his future son-in-law, George Kerbawy. According to my first cousin Minnie Kerbawy, the daughter of Maheba, George and Maheba ran away upon landing in New York. Assaf ran after them commanding them to halt, but to no avail. This story is not factually accurate as Maheba and George were married in 1896, but it probably does reflect Assaf's attitude and personality.

The boat that brought the contingent of Kfeirians to New York was The California, only 300 feet long and 38 feet wide, very small for a North Atlantic passenger vessel. These dimensions are less than the riverboats that presently cruise European rivers. If the seas were not absolutely calm on that June passage in 1895, the passengers would have suffered greatly, particularly because there were as many as 1250 passengers aboard. The maximum speed of the ship was only 10 knots, or about 12 mpg. It was an exclusively "steerage" vessel: that is, "third class" only. The ship, commissioned in 1882, was powered by coal, but also utilized sails when possible.

Grandfather Assaf, along with most of the Kferian group, came to Toledo. He was only there for four years. His wife, my grandmother Numnum Abou Jamra, passed away in 1897. At the home of Minnie Kerbawy in Blissfield, I once spied a snapshot of him in a suit with vest and hat. He looked short and very uncomfortable. His intention to earn a living by being a peddler was made more difficult when his daughter Maheba married and could not help him as he had intended. Young Maheba would have picked up the English language much quicker than her 36-year old father.

My knowledge of Assaf is based mainly on my mother's recollections, which were not positive. Today he would be labeled a sexist, but in his time, his behavior was more or less common, if not normal. That is, he drank more than he should, played cards, and expected his young daughters to do a woman's work in spite of their young age. He withdrew daughter Rahija from primary school, after only two years of instruction, on his return to Kfeir in 1899. Her job at eight years of age was to run the household, which consisted of Assaf, Rahija and baby Della, four years younger than her sister. Rajiha cooked, kept house, fetched water from the village well, and made sure that Assad had alcohol during his frequent nightly card games. Assaf once punished the girls because they had fallen asleep and failed to meet his needs. Some of other men chided Assaf for his insensitivity.

Sometime after Assef's return he married a second time to a woman my mother adored. Her name was Muliki, which meant Queen. She had a son who is seen in the photo. It must have been a great relief to my mother to have a stepmother in the house to relieve her of some responsibility. My mother had kind words for Muliki, and she was disappointed that after a while, Muliki took her son and returned to her home in Beirut, tired of Assaf's abuse. I have often wondered if this was a formal marriage or merely a housekeeping arrangement. On my mother's trip to America in 1911, she stayed several days with Muliki in Beirut until her ship arrived.

Numnum abou Jamra
1865-1897

Assaf married Numnum abou Jamra when she was only 14. Their first child, Maheba, was born when Numnum was 15. Subsequently she had more children when she was 18 (Sam), 22 (Jasper), 26 (Rahija), and 30 (Della). My mother Rahija says that Numnum had red hair. Uncle Jasper reported that she suffered for ten years and ultimately died from a tumor at the age of 32.

Rahija tells the story of asking her mother Numnum to wipe her nose, a request that earned the child a slap on the face. Rahija remembered the incident with sadness and puzzlement. However, when you consider that a single woman is raising a family of six children, and is in progressively ill health, you develop understanding and sympathy. My mother remembers Numnum's funeral, although she was only six years old. She said her body was placed in the ground with only a sheet around it. There was no money for a casket. During my first visit to Kfeir, I visited the graveyard, where only a few markers were there to identify those buried, such being the lack of wealth of the villagers.

This is the only photograph of children of Assef and Numnum Saad taken together, about 1953 in Columbus, Ohio. Standing, From Left Della, Jasper, Rahija; Seated, Sam, Maheba.

Maheba Saad Kerbawy
1880 – 1960

Maheba, the oldest child, had the true bearing of a family matriarch. This resulted from a long life married to a stable and responsible husband, and from having many descendants. By the turn of the 21st century there were six generations of her offspring. The family home in Blissfield, Michigan was a large brick home, still standing, with a large kitchen where good smells emanated. Maheba and George (1873-1965) had seven children, two boys and five girls. I admired them all. Four of the five girls all lived into their late 90s: Elizabeth (95), Minnie (97), Nellie (98), and Gracie (98). Niemee, the fifth female, died before her second birthday. The two sons had shorter but still long lives: Alex (87) and Haford (86).

Nellie Kerbawy Wakeam lived for years in London, Ontario, before moving to Toledo and eventually to Miami, where we visited several times. At age 95, Nellie was still driving and she shopped while wearing high heels! When we talked on the telephone, Nellie would always ask about my wife, and children, and sisters. She always remembered us. Nellie, Gracie, and Minnie were the three sisters I remembered best, and they had the same graciousness, inner beauty and strength that was characteristic of their mother Maheba.

Minnie never married, living in the family house all her life. She became the manager and then owner of the general store in Blissfield that her father George started. Nellie told me that Uncle Sam Saad brought my mother Rahija to Blissfield from Kentucky a very short while after she arrived in the United States. (Sam and Jasper shared an apartment with no space for their sister.) Rahija, tall, beautiful and with great physical bearing, was told to walk into the kitchen where Maheba was cooking and say nothing. Maheba, who had left Kfeir when Rahija was four years old, turned to see this stranger. But it took only a minute or so for her to recognize her sister. I delight in this story because it is easy to feel the amazement of the moment—the tears that welled up, the laughter that followed, and the rush of deep feelings of joy and happiness.

Minnie, ten years younger than Rahija, says they slept in the same bed, and she recalled that Rahija was "a laughing woman." Rahija stayed in Blissfield for several months having found a job as a seamstress in the local fur factory. The sewing skills learned at that time served her well when she had a family of five girls to clothe.

Rahija was living in Blissfield, when she was "courted" by Abraham Bassett, who lived four miles north of Blissfield on a farm. Maheba was the matchmaker. To be "courted" probably meant that they saw each other when Abraham came to visit the Kerbawy family, having some brief conversations. Abraham asked George Kerbawy for permission to marry Rahija. For some time, Rahija demurred, but George kept urging Rahija to say yes, and eventually she did, explaining, "George kept talking until he made up my mind."

When Rahija married Abraham Bassett, February 2, 1914, they married in Maheba and George's house. The day before on February 1st, Maheba's oldest daughter, Elizabeth, married Albert Jamra. Elizabeth, six years younger than Rahija, objected to a double wedding. The wedding on the next day was officiated by the same Orthodox priest.

These stories signify the closeness of our family to the Kerbawy family, a closeness that has lasted more than a century.

My feelings toward George Kerbawy were not as warm as they were toward my Aunt Maheba. George, like many Kfeirian (Lebanese) men of the time, probably felt boys should be seen and not heard, and young men should always be in deference to older men. My father, Abraham, was an exception to such behavior.

Sam Saad
1883 – 1973

My Uncle Sam Saad was sometimes listed on official documents as Samuel or in the Arabic form, Sleiman (of which there are deviant spellings). Uncle Sam was somewhat like Uncle George Kerbawy in that he did not make any effort to have a special relationship with me. He had a physical presence because he was shorter than my father and a little thicker in the middle. He always wore a bushy moustache and his cigar smoking gave him a special aroma.

Sam lived in Pikeville, Kentucky, where he first ran a grocery store and later a liquor and beer store. Also in  Pikeville was his brother Jasper. Sam, reportedly, became very attached to Jasper's first daughter Pauline, born in 1914. Pauline tragically died at the age of three years, three months when her dress caught fire as she reached for a fruit. Sam never again allowed himself to be emotionally close to children. While Uncle Sam was not unkind to me, he was not particularly warm; the death of Pauline may explain why.

Maheba had worked as a peddler and had saved money (reportedly $300), which she used, in part, to bring Sam to the United States. Once Sam arrived it became his responsibility to help bring his younger siblings to the United States.

Sam immigrated to the United States in 1901 at the age of 18, earning his living as a peddler. He came to Pikeville in 1904 because it had only one grocery store. When his brother Jasper arrived in 1905, Jasper came directly to Pikeville to work with Sam in the grocery store. In 1905 Sam was 22 and Jasper was 18. To avoid discrimination they decided that when they were in the store they should only speak English. In the store they introduced oranges and Brazil Nuts, which were known then by the racially insensitive name "niggertoes." Pikeville, unlike Williamson, 30 miles away, where my family grew up, was an ethnically pure locale. Williamson was ethnically diverse with many foreigners including Italians, Armenians, Syrians, Jews, and Muslims and was a more tolerant community than Pikeville.

The grocery business was successful and over the years

expanded to sell other items, eventually morphing into Saad's Liquor And Beer. A contemporary photograph shows the store also sold whiskey, wine, pipes, ice cream, tobacco, candy, novelties, etc. The exterior of the building stands today virtually unchanged from a century ago, now housing a lawyer's office.

At one point after my father and mother married (1914), Sam brought my father into partnership, which happened in late 1915. But by May 1916, Abraham moved his family to Williamson, where he established "A. J. Bassett Fruit & Confectionary."

Sometime before Sam married Muntaha, he had fathered a child, but Sam refused to marry the woman because she was "loose." Later, the woman would bring the child to the store and have the child address Sam as "Daddy!" It was an embarrassment to Sam, but he persevered. One can imagine the gossip this caused!

When Sam sold his grocery he and Muntaha retired to Brooklyn, New York. I remember the address: 9001 Ridge Blvd.

In the very late 1960s or early 1970s, Sam arrived unannounced at his sister Della's house in Charleston, West Virginia, saying that Muntaha was treating him badly. After a time, he returned. Events of this nature are quickly hidden from view and discussed only in whispered tones.

Sam died in the summer of 1973 and was buried September 4 in Brooklyn.

Muntaha
1898 - 1982

Sam Saad's wife Muntaha (spelled Mintaha on census records) emigrated in 1907 from Damascus, Syria. This had to be an arranged marriage where neither party knew much about the other. Very little is known about Muntaha except that it was said by Aunt Clara "she was not a nice person." Once, Muntaha accused Jasper's wife Clara of rolling her baby buggy with baby Paul in it, in front of Sam's store, where Muntaha clerked, "just to spite" Muntaha. Clara said she would be frightened to do that for fear Muntaha would do something bad to the baby.

There are pictures of Muntaha showing her to be fashionably dressed. Her home in Pikeville was immaculate, and we children were always chased out of the house for fear we would break something or track in dirt. I never remember having a meal in her house although we made many trips to Pikeville. I avoided her having never heard her speak a kind word.

Perhaps some of my descendants who are reading this will search for more information on my Aunt Muntaha. You know, I think that is the first time that I combined the word "aunt" with the name "Muntaha!"

Jasper Isperidon Saad
1887-1978

J asper was probably happy to immigrate to America at age 18 in part to escape his father. He says he was required to give money he had earned to his father, and to kneel before him and kiss his hand. Jasper had an excellent command of the English language and had excellent penmanship. This suggests that he had maximum schooling in Kfeir and explains why he was able do some teaching in Kfeir. It was also said that Jasper went to Damascus to study photography but another report says that Sam sponsored Jasper in learning photography.

It was as a photographer that he made his living for many years, having studios both in Pikeville and later in Williamson. We are blessed to have many portraits, obviously taken in the

Saad Studio. On several occasions, the entire family had a portrait taken in our home in Williamson. My sister Lorraine worked for Uncle Jasper, running the studio when Jasper was away and learning to tint black and white photographs. I can recall people coming to the studio to pick up their photos, which were "not ready yet." I think, in time, he lost interest in the nitty-gritty work of the dark room. But early photographs of his children were very artistic.

Uncle Jasper was a very gentle, sensitive, but not practical man. Those were the words of his wife Clara. I agree with the assessment that he was kind, gentle, sensitive, and loving. I knew him better than my other uncles because he lived a good number of years in Williamson, having separated (but not divorced) from Clara, who continued to live in Pikeville. For many years, his photographic studio was adjacent to Bassett's Confectionery Store, across from the N&W depot. In the 1930s, during the depression, my father had installed slot machines in the rear of the Confectionary store. I watched Jasper playing the slots, and I had the notion that he was addicted to gambling. It would not be inconsistent with the relationship of our family that if Jasper lost money on the slots, the money would be returned to him. Jasper also owned and operated a movie theatre on 2nd Avenue. Sam had sponsored him in the venture, and Jasper once said he regretted not staying in this business. The movie theatre's auditorium was smaller than that of the Cinderella Theatre, which gave Uncle Jasper formidable competition.

The charge of Jasper not being a practical person comes from his wife Clara. Once, Clara said, she gave Jasper $2 to go grocery shopping but he came home without groceries. When asked, he said he gave the money to a destitute person. Clara protested that his family was almost destitute, but Jasper was hurt by the rebuke, saying, "I thought you would be proud of me."

On another occasion, Jasper bought a new violin and violin lessons, even though at the time he had four children. She said they endured his practicing, but after a while he quit the violin and sold it for much less than he paid.

Jasper and Clara had six children. In addition to little Pauline who did not see her fourth birthday, Aletha died in 1933 at age seven from appendicitis. The four remaining children, all very bright, were very close to my family. Lucille (b. 1917) graduated from Williamson High School. She and my sister Selma were of the same age and very close friends. Lucille had a remarkable career in Pikeville as Post Mistress, newspaper columnist and radio host. She was known throughout the county.

John Isper (b. 1919) had a career in the United State Army. Paul, (b. 1929) was friend to my sister Lorraine and to me. He became a successful lawyer in Tampa, Florida, and once ran for a seat in the United State Congress.

Rose (b. 1939), the mother of three girls, has lived in Frankfort, Kentucky, Washington, DC, Tampa, Florida, and now in Pikeville, Kentucky. Sharon and I once offered an opportunity for Rose to live with us while attending college in Missouri where I was teaching.

Clara Sword Saad
1896-1992

Clara, as a teenager, was deemed the most beautiful young lady in Pike County, Kentucky. As Jasper was a very good looking young man you could understand their initial attraction to each other. Clara recalls that in 1912 when she was 16, she came to Saad Studio to have her picture taken. Jasper wanted to take Clara's picture with a cloth draped on her shoulders, which was customary in those days, but Clara refused. The cloth was draped over her shoulders and blouse, but in the photograph, the blouse is seen. Clara thinks her modesty may have been an enticement to Jasper. They were married February 14, 1914 when Clara was 18 and Jasper 27. The wedding was 12 days following that of Rahija and Abraham.

I visited Aunt Clara several times. The last time I recall how she dressed up for me. She wore a sweatshirt with a colorful scarf around her neck and a beret on her head. She had on lipstick. She was pretty. And she was proud that on her meager social security income she had saved $300,000, to bequeath to her children.

Della Saad McCarus
1895-1981

Della was four years old before she met her father. Assef had departed Kfeir for America in June 1895 and Della was born August 17, 1895. Today, one finds it difficult to imagine a man leaving his seven-month pregnant wife with three young children to raise. Presumably he did earn money as a peddler in Ohio and Michigan, but in the late 19th century, how did one safely transmit money to a small mountain village, far from a city center, in a country of the Ottoman Empire?

Della immigrated to the United States in 1914 at the age of 18. She married 28-year old Nasseph McCarus, February 10,

1918 in Williamson, the home of her older sister Rahija. Della and Nasseph settled in Charleston, the state capitol.

Della and Nasseph produced six children, four boys and two girls. They are Mitchell (b. 1919), Edward (b. 1920), Ernest (b. 1922), Ramez (b. 1925), Mary Frances (b. 1926) and Norma (b. 1932). Because the dates of birth of the McCarus family closely match those of my family, there was a special bonding between the families. The families saw each other at the annual Kfeirian Reunion, but travelling from Williamson to Charleston was a long and difficult journey on the West Virginia highways, discouraging visiting as often as would have been desired.

Uncle Nasseph was to me as so many of the Lebanese men I have described earlier. In fairness to him, there was little opportunity for a mature man to get to know a young person. It is ironic that Nasseph's birth and death years are the same as my father (1885-1949).

My mother suffered her fatal stroke in Charleston while visiting Della. Her daughter Mary Francis reports that the night before the stroke, Rahija and Della were up late recalling incidents from their early life, causing them to erupt over and over with gales of laughter. Della died December 14, 1981, just 18 months after that raucous night of laughter.

My sister Selma and I left Columbus to attend the funeral but turned back after traveling 45 miles because of a very heavy snow storm. In Charleston, the funeral was delayed one day. Because of my admiration for the McCarus family, I attended the funeral of Mary Francis in 2012.

FIVE SISTERS

Upper Arlington, July 1947 From Left: Lorraine, Wadad, Gladys, Selma

Gladys (1915-2002) was Papa's girl, sharing his body type and personality. As the oldest child he depended on her as a confidant and to take charge of the business as needed.

When Lorraine and I were young, Gladys was our advocate, once arguing we should have a weekly allowance. We considered the 25 cents we received a fair amount, but nothing like the $5 Johnny Wheeler reportedly received. When I was in high school, she bought me a sport coat, which I was too embarrassed to wear because of its vivid multi colors. I had the coat dyed thinking it would become a solid dark blue, but it turned out to be very much like a black watch plaid. I loved that coat and wore it for years.

Gladys loved books and for years subscribed to the Book of the Month Club. She was both meticulous in personal possessions and overwhelmed with collections of papers and things. When Gladys was in an automobile accident I had to find her insurance papers to present to the hospital. Her purse was immaculate; her wallet was like a filing cabinet with everything in its place. While her house was sometimes "junky," the papers were stacked around the room in neat piles.

I loved Gladys for her sense of humor, but more so because of her love for me. She was sometimes my surrogate mother.

Selma (1916-2012) was Mama's girl, the one who learned to cook Arabic food, and the one who best absorbed Mama's stories

 and culture. They lived together for many years; Selma was Mama's chauffeur and Mama was Selma's baby sitter. Mama was storyteller and Selma was genealogist. She was the family's athlete. She was the most coordinated and had the best figure. Others always saw Selma as cute, petite, energetic and gracious being very liberal in her gift giving. She was a Red Cross certified swimming instructor and lifeguard, and a tennis and basketball player. She was always ready for a competitive game. Once during a 4th of July gathering, we were playing volleyball in our back yard, and Selma, then in her 70's played with those much younger, even though her mobility was limited.

I would also describe her as adventuresome. While touring in Syria, very rough waters made the proposed trip to Arwad Island risky. No one wished to go in the small boat except Selma, age 82, who said she would go if someone would join her. No one did.

Selma was my Band Director in Junior High School, and was responsible for my playing the trombone. We traveled to distant West Virginia cities for band competitions, and I came to dislike going. Selma always over packed and I was the one who contended with her extra suitcases. Over packing was a life long attribute.

Wadad (1917-2001) was the family beauty. She knew the most about makeup and hair styling and finding stylish clothes. The

time spent preparing for special occasions always resulted in "wow" moments from the family. However, she could be carefree about her dress around the house. She often wore tie shoes with heels, with her feet in mismatched anklet socks.

During World War II, she worked in Detroit in a plant building armaments and was commended for her good work. After the war, unmarried and without nearby prospects, Wadad spent considerable energy making her self available to potential mates, finally meeting her husband, Jim Boyfysil.

Alice (1921-2011) was the brainy one in the family, the one most able to deal with abstract thoughts, and the most adventurous. I have described Alice's characteristics, and our special relationship in the eulogy delivered at her Celebration of Life service. [See Section IX, page 227]

Lorraine, (1929-   ) 21 months older than me, was not a childhood playmate. Being two grade levels ahead, her classmates were her playmates. An early memory of my sister was when at the school grounds I fell, face first, bloodying my nose. Lorraine came to console me and stem the flow of blood. I remember that special and surprising moment as the first time I felt she was my sister.

Lorraine as a teenager was energetic and funny, with lots of girl friends, and in high school drew significant attention

from the boys. When she met and married Bill Scott it was with my whole-hearted approval, a man I saw as a big brother. Lorraine had great drive to better herself, and after giving birth to two sons, returned to school to earn her Bachelors, Masters, and Doctorate degrees. Our relationship became and remained very strong from the time of our college years.

IX | REMEMBRANCES

REMEMBERING MY DEAR SISTER GLADYS
Gladys Shumla Bassett Parlette
1915 - 2002

*This is the text of an email letter sent to my extended family
reporting on the memorial service for Gladys.*

A small memorial service was held for Gladys on Sunday, April 28, 2002 at Trinity Episcopal Church in Columbus. My sisters Lorraine and Selma arranged Arabic food for a reception after the memorial service. Abe and Selma gave remembrances of Gladys during the service. A small number of family friends, and acquaintances of Selma, attended the service.

Ironically, April 28 is the birthday of our father, Abraham Joseph Bassett, who was born in 1885. Gladys and Papa were quite close and he depended on her, perhaps more so than the other children, particularly in terms of running his businesses. Gladys and Papa shared body type and facial structure, both had the same color eyes and both enjoyed the company of other people.

Abraham, Gladys, and Uncle Sam on the farm, c. 1946

Gladys was not a person to complain of others or of her own situation. Until later years she lived a relatively healthy life, seldom sick. Her medical visits were all related to weight loss, which was a life-long concern. It was from Gladys that I first learned the word "metabolism." And yet it is ironic that most of the pictures we have of Gladys show her with a trim body.

With relish I recall August 1, 1964, the day Sharon and I

departed Columbus for Tacoma, Washington. The entire family spent an extra two hours parked in front of the house at 132 East 11th Avenue, talking and joking. Gladys was planning to leave that night for a vacation in Boston, and had prepared for the trip by losing weight. I recall she wore a black dress and was very attractive. Gladys was effervescent that day, a natural feeling when you feel good about yourself.

Gladys loved books and reading and she enjoyed people. Her declining years began with an unfortunate automobile accident when she was driving from Columbus to Huntington for a Kfeirian Reunion. She sustained a severe cut to her mouth which healed in due time. The damage to her knee was more severe from which she never fully recovered. It led to less physical activity, which lead to weight gain, which led to fewer contacts with friends and family. When we finally were able to bring Gladys into an assisted living situation, she was in poor physical condition. However, the last three years of her life were improved greatly with medical attention and care to basic needs. With that improvement, laughter and sparkle returned.

Gladys was known and liked by all the caregivers. They enjoyed her humor and her reactions to them. At Wesley Ridge, she liked to sit in her wheel chair by the nurse's station to "direct traffic" and observe the happenings. When I visited Gladys, she always greeted me with a smile, and we never parted without laughter.

I cannot conclude this message without noting the loving care that Selma provided Gladys in the past fifteen years. They were virtual twins as only 11 months separated their birth. Selma devoted many hours each week helping Gladys cope. Until Gladys entered Wesley Ridge, Selma was the only person Gladys would allow to be close to her. Gladys—and the family—owe a great deal to Selma for her incredible effort and loving care.

REMEMBERING MY DEAR SISTER ALICE
Alice Tamam Bassett Rutherdale
1921-2011

*This is the eulogy I delivered at the Celebration of Life for Alice
on Sunday, May 29, 2011 in Sacramento, California.*

To celebrate the life of Alice Tamam Bassett is why we are
here this morning. Alice's spirit is but a little way above
our heads. If you will listen carefully, you can hear her say,
"Thank you, My Family, for being here today."

Her long life was at times exciting, challenging, productive
and difficult. She was in turn a dutiful daughter, an
excellent student, a dedicated mother and wife, a musician, a
cryptologist and a biology teacher. She was our mother, our
grandmother, our great-grandmother, our mother-in-law, our
sister and our inspiration.

Alice was born Tuesday, October 11, 1921 between 2:00 and 4:00 p.m., at 410 Dickinson Street, Williamson, West Virginia. I was born in the same town, same house, and almost exactly nine years later in 1930. We were both born under the sign of Libra.

My relationship with my sister Alice contributed in important ways to my development. Her lifelong encouragement inspired me to look forward and to work hard. She was my mentor, my pacesetter, and an inspiration.

Alice was one of five older sisters—the fourth of five girls in our family—but perhaps the one whom I thought of as my "big sister," the sister who instructed and guided me. When I wrote to her in 1987, I said, "you took me under your wings."

One of my earlier memories was when I was about six and Alice 15. Lorraine and I were walking side by side with Alice when we came to a ladder on the sidewalk, forcing us to break ranks and walk on either side of the ladder. To do so was to cause bad luck and in order to break the hex that would befall us for being split apart, both persons must simultaneously say the magic phrase "bread and butter." But Alice went one step further to say the magic words were "brown bread and butter."

With respect to good manners, she said I should always speak first to an older person, increasingly difficult to do these days. And she told me to always open a door for a girl or a woman.

When I was seven and Alice 16, I thrilled to see her marching in the high school band. Her instrument was the largest in the band—the bass horn. I marveled that she could carry such a heavy load, not knowing the horn was hollow. But it was heavy enough that our mother Rahija built a shoulder pad to make her load less of a burden.

It greatly pleased our father that Alice was an excellent student and a huge help to him by working at Bassett's Confectionary. When Papa suffered a heart attack in 1938, Alice ran the confectionary for three weeks, opening it up in the morning and closing it at night. She was 16 years old.

At 17 years and seven months of age, in May 1939, she graduated from Williamson High School, and Papa rewarded her with a graduation gift of $35. Alice's first impulse was to buy a lifetime subscription to the Readers Digest, but Papa suggested a better use for the money. The gift was applied to summer term tuition at Concord College in Athens, West Virginia. Alice never again lived at home except for brief vacations from school.

At the end of her freshman year at Concord, she enrolled for summer school at the University of Michigan, returning to Concord in the fall. Amazingly, her music teachers encouraged her to transfer to Marshall College in Huntington, West Virginia, to take advantage of a much stronger music program. Can you imagine a situation where teachers encourage their best student to study at another institution? Alice did transfer and subsequently graduated with a Bachelor's of Music Education degree, three years out of high school.

Without missing a beat, she began graduate studies that summer at Michigan and then accepted a one-year teaching contract at Cassopolis Michigan High School. She returned to the University of Michigan in June of 1943 and in February 1944 received a Master of Music degree. Amazingly, at age 22 years and four months, she had a Bachelor's degree, a Master's degree, and one year of teaching experience.

I would like to place Alice's education in the context of education for women in the first half of the last century and in the context of her family's values. When I began my teaching career in 1960, many of my students were the first to go to college. That is even true today and it was especially true in the 1930s.

My father had only three years of schooling and my mother only two years. However, both could read and write Arabic and both taught themselves to read and write in English. My mother Rahija learned English by studying her children's schoolbooks, and that is the way she learned to play the piano. Among my most prized possessions are their letters and notes written to me. During the depression, unemployment was very high, and income was very low. Educating girls was not a high priority, except in my family.

All six of the Bassett children were either born during or graduated from high school in the depression years. Among them they earned one two-year teaching certificate, four bachelor's degrees, three master's degrees and two doctorates. Of the six, five became teachers. Alice, arguably the brightest of the six, is a product of two remarkable parents who esteemed education for their children.

The spring after graduation from Michigan, Alice did two remarkable things. First, she became a substitute biology teacher at Williamson High School, and she joined the Army. In one of the letters she wrote to me while I suffered my Army basic training, she bemoaned that her basic training was exceedingly boring. However she was never again bored as her next army assignment was to the Signal Corps Intelligence unit in Washington, DC. She became a cryptologist; only the brightest of the bright could hope to have such an elevated assignment. She eventually became a Sergeant, but was discharged three weeks after earning her third stripe; however, she was immediately rehired as a civilian to continue her work as a code breaker. Her high civil service rating was well paying.

It was in Washington that she met Jack Rutherdale. They were married February 1946 and by the end of the year were living in California. When I was 16, my parents gave me permission that summer to visit Alice and Jack; I stayed nearly two months, living in San Carlos and El Cerrito in married student's house for University of California Berkeley students.

Traveling alone at a young age was not unusual in our family. When Alice was barely 14, Papa allowed Alice to travel alone to visit Bassett relatives in Welch, West Virginia, a family of all boys close to the age of my sisters. She wrote to her sister Selma, in October 1935, "she spent the weekend in Welch and had plenty of fun." Selma was sworn to never reveal the greatest secret of that weekend: "I've determined to marry Clement Bassett . . . but he doesn't know it yet."

I saw Alice as bold and adventuresome, extremely intelligent, very positive and gracious. I admired my sister for going off to college, going off to war, instructing me in Emily Post dictums, teaching me to play bridge, and for welcoming me into her home on many occasions. She was always glad to see me, and always equipped with kind words of encouragement. I think she liked me.

When I went to college and later after college to the service, we corresponded frequently. She saved many of my letters and I saved hers. In the past few weeks I have read through those letters.

When I was in the Army she encouraged me to "be the best I could be" which may be where the Army found their slogan. She also taught me her method of memorizing numbers, such as my army serial number. She said, "mine was melodious." All I had to do was to set it to music, letting the numbers correspond to notes on the treble clef---do re me fa so. 52 235 055 = So, Re, Re, Me, So, X, So, So.

When we discussed our tastes in music and she told me that Beethoven's late quartets were perhaps the most sublime of all music. That encouraged me to listen carefully to these works and to come to total agreement about their sublimity and her musical judgment.

In 1953, when I was in the Army in Okinawa, and Alice was the mother of three children, we had several exchanges discussing Ayn Rand's "The Fountainhead." I extolled Howard Roark's individualism, but Alice brought me down to earth making me focus on the superficiality of the main characters in the melodramatic story.

In June and July of 1953, Alice wrote to me eight times,

a letter a week. In one letter she said, "Your letter was an excellent justification of your education . . . you made me proud of you...." In a letter I wrote to her I said, "Your answers to my questions were beautiful, and intelligent.... You did a fabulous analysis." Alice and I corresponded even when she was at Agnew State Hospital in 1958, telling me that she was progressing well in her treatment. This positive attitude was characteristic of Alice, for she always said, in response to my inquiry about her health, that she was doing just fine.

In Alice's years following her illness, she was most fortunate in having a family that did not abandon her but continued to love and help her when she was most in need. The love that Alice's children felt toward her has been transmitted to their children. The fact that so many of you have come to his memorial is a testament to the love and respect you have for Alice. I wish to acknowledge a few of the many things you have done for my sister.

For example, you gathered in Los Altos to clean the house, clear the garden and to make repairs, some of which were major.

You had a role in convincing Alice to answer the telephone so we could communicate with her. Tom encouraged the family to make regular telephone contact. Do you recall the matrix he prepared asking each of us to call Alice on certain days of the month?

As her conservator, Jan has spent many hours dealing with Alice's financial affairs, writing long detailed accounts to the court describing Alice's situation, the sum total of which are a valuable history.

Nancy traveled to Los Altos many times over three decades to spend overnights with her mother and to see to her needs. Alice was never interested in seeing doctors, but Nancy convinced her to see a physician in Los Altos and again in Sacramento. This was done through gentle but persistent persuasion.

Nancy and Alice traveled together to Kfeirian Reunions in West Virginia, Las Vegas, and Ohio. They also visited Jan and Jeff in Juneau. In Sacramento, Nancy and Alice had a weekly visit to the Westminster Presbyterian Church for concerts and for lunch afterwards. And they played bridge at the senior center and enjoyed frequent visits to the art museum and parks.

The last three years of Alice's life in Sacramento were happy ones. Tom and Nancy found the wonderful house on M Street with the large kitchen window that looked out on East Portal Park. Alice delighted in watching the activity on her street and in the park: mothers with strollers, joggers, skaters and bikers, picnickers, old folks and young lovers. She loved her lemon tree and the stoop where she could sun herself.

Thanks to the family visitors to M Street who made it easy for Alice to live happily and to Tom and Nancy for their daily visits. I have thanked Tom a hundred times for all he has done for his mother-in-law. Has any son ever treated a mother better than Tom treated Alice?

Alice's last words will always be embedded in our memory, coming in response to the caretakers asking if she wanted to bathe: "Yes," said Alice, "I want to look good because my family is coming."

REMEMBERING MY BROTHER-IN -LAW JACK
John (Jack) Wiley Rutherdale, Jr.
1924 – 2010

These comments were written for the celebration of life ceremony for Jack Rutherdale. When I could not attend, my grand niece and Jack's granddaughter Rose Griffith read the comments.

Jack Rutherdale was my brother before he was my brother-in-law.

I first met Jack in 1945, when Alice and he came to Williamson during their Christmas furlough from Army service in Arlington, Virginia. I was 15 and Jack was 22. I bonded with Jack immediately; he became my surrogate brother and the first of my brothers-in-law.

Whatever words were spoken or ideas expressed are long forgotten except for the reaction that came with my bragging that Williamson was the site of the world's "largest broom handle factory." I can hear Jack's laughter now; it is a laugh heard thousands of times since that moment.

In the years that followed, I was always warmly welcomed into his home with Alice and later with Anne, his second wife. My first visit in the summer of 1947 found me sharing their bedroom, sleeping on a cot in their student housing in El Cerrito when they were both Berkeley students.

There were many subsequent visits over the years, and I was always welcomed to sleep in their house, eat at their table, wash clothes and car, and play with their children.

After my Army service, I moved to California, staying with Jack and Alice until I found a job in the City and a place to live. Two years later, I found myself in Paris without sufficient funds to live until the arrival of my first GI Bill stipend. Jack sent a check by return mail to tide me over, and he waited silently until month by month the loan was repaid.

In the many years since, I have visited with Jack and Anne in their home and traveled with them to France, Spain, Tunisia, London and Paris. The graciousness, warmth, and quiet humanity first discovered 64 years ago, never wavered and were never held in reserve. The laugh never changed nor has my love for my brother Jack.

MY UNCLE FRANK'S SEPTEMBER SONG

Written in 1989, following a visit with Uncle Frank in his home in Detroit.

Uncle Frank was unshaven with perhaps a two-day growth. It was the first time I had seen him this way and it was an immediate signal to me that Aunt Eugenia was no longer there.

When he came to the door, soon after my knocking, he was wearing a khaki-colored cap and a blue-checked Dacron jacket. I had invited him to lunch and he was waiting for me and he was hungry.

We drove to Steve's Backroom, his favorite restaurant, where Mediterranean cuisine is served. Parking close to the side door, he said, "No, you can't park in the disabled space. Do you have a permit?"

As we walked on the sloping sidewalk approaching the restaurant, I had to take his arm to keep him from falling off the edge. It was as if he were rolling off a slanted table, no longer able to compensate for the lack of a level piece of ground. His steps came very slowly, each foot advancing a few inches in front of the other. The threshold to the restaurant door was only a half-inch high but I wondered if it would cause him to stumble.

We ate in relative silence. On the drive home Frank talked, separating new thoughts with meaningful pauses.
"I wanted to die first. It isn't fair."
"The Creator must have something for me to do."
"Eugenia said it is easier to die than to live. She was right. I'm not afraid of dying."

"While you are here, you lose a brother, a sister, a wife. It is hard."

At home, Frank sat in his recliner, head back against the pillow, eyes shut. In our conversation there were long pauses between thoughts and some pauses lasting several minutes. Amazingly, after one such long pause—a thought, interrupted in mid-sentence—continued with the second part of the sentence. Where did the mind go, what images floated across? I cannot enter his twilight zone.

The mouth drooped, and then came a real slumber, a deep sleep. From the semiconscious state of relaxation to a deep sleep in an instant, induced partly from ennui and partly from the digestion of lunch.

As he slept, I studied Frank. His body weight was down. Gone from his face was the fat, but the skin was remarkably taut for a 94-year old man. There were very few wrinkles. A vein crept across the skull from ear to ear as if it was a canal crossing the face of Mars. He had black marks on lips, like chewing tobacco. Then came a series of most gentle snores.

Frank wore a clean, faded, blue and peach plaid shirt, buttoned at the top; a black ballpoint pen sat in a shirt pocket. He wore soft brown deerskin shoes.

He awakened. There was a major effort to pull himself up from a lounged position on the recliner, to be able to bring the telephone directory into the proper distance for his tri-focal glasses.

I took the glasses to the bathroom to clean the lens.

A tape recorder sat in the car. I felt ashamed to bring it in to record the feeble, soft voice of a dying, lonely, heartbroken man who fervently wished to die and didn't know that his wish was being granted.

There are long pauses while the mind's computer searched his memory bank for the first name of a grandmother or the first name of five paternal aunts. An error message said, "No file found."

"I had known Jean (Eugenia) since 1927 . . . 63 years." There was a slow motion movement with the back of the hand to wipe a tear from the eye.

He waved for me to reach an important memento of Eugenia: it was a photograph of her svelte, trim, sophisticated sister standing before a 1920 long hooded Duisenberg Roadster with its top down and rumble seat open. The inscription read, "To my Dearest Twin Sister, I miss you so much, Irene." Twin sister Irene wore a hat and gloves; a shiny print rayon dress falling just below her knees revealed shiny silk stockings.

And then another memento: It is an autographed picture of a young, handsome Charlton Heston, inscribed "To Jean . . ." Frank took a 25-minute nap and then had a startled awakening as he turned to see me sitting there. His reaction seemed to be a surprised "who are you" followed by a quick remembrance. "Yes, it is you. Excuse me, I was resting my eyes."

The house was neat. There was no junk, no accumulation; it was as if Jean were still there. Maybe, I think, it was Frank who taught Jean to be neat. Near the front door there was a three-tiered table, with knickknacks and figurines on the bottom two shelves and a large purple-flowered plant on the top.

In his semi-sleep, a coin purse filled with pennies, nickels and dimes was withdrawn from his trouser pocket, felt, opened, closed, and returned.

VICTOR HABIB BASSETT
April 21, 1920 - June 1, 2007

My first cousin Victor died alone without close family, as he had lived in his octogenarian years. I was the one family member with whom Victor felt comfortable. We had maintained a relationship over the years by writing, telephoning and emailing. I wrote this account of some of his history and his last days to send to those family members who knew him or knew of him. This is my way to preserve the life and memory of a very interesting and good man.

The editors of Buckeye, the Napoleon High school annual of 1938 were perspicacious in their description of Victor Habib Bassett. An "intellectual giant" they wrote, associating

him with the term *cogito ergo sum* [I think, therefore I am] and identifying him as a young person interested in philosophy and abstract thought. "In reading," they wrote, he was "as voracious as a shark," and "with a glint of iron in his eyes, but never doubt, nor yet surprise." Victor's yearbook picture reinforces this description, particularly as he was the only male in the graduating class of 84 students to wear glasses. The greatest insight in that brief yearbook description was the last seven words attributed to Victor: "why should life all labor be."

Vic once told me that his real life began at five o'clock in the afternoon; when the workday was done and the paycheck earned, it was time to grow by pursuing one's special interests. Never married, and with no family obligation, Victor was able to pursue a great variety of interests. He could not be labeled a dilettante because his devotion to his many interests was measured in years.

Victor's main life's work was with the Department of Defense, first beginning government service at Wright Patterson Air Force Base in Dayton, Ohio as an "Industrial Specialist" from 1951 to 1955. He then moved to Washington, D.C. to take a position with the Bureau of Naval Weapons as an Aircraft Cost Estimator (1955-1962) and then to the Institute of Defense Analyses as a Cost Analyst until retirement.

Because he had applied for a "Top Secret" clearance, he had in his personal files a detailed history of where he lived, where he worked, and where he went to school. Once he spent a night in jail in Columbus, Ohio for driving 30 M.P.H. in a 25 M.P.H. zone! Throughout his life he was a meticulous record keeper and list maker. He left a series of day planners even for the last seven years of his life, although many days carried the notation, "nothing happened."

Between graduating from high school in 1938 and entering Ohio State in 1942, he had a variety of jobs including a "tool room apprentice," a "lathe hand," and a "tool designer." He first majored in Industrial Design but this major did not suit him well, and after one year entered the US Army as a private. After basic training he was recommended for OCS—Officer Candidate School—becoming a second lieutenant and serving in the Philippines in the Army Air Corp.

After military service from 1943 to 1946, he reentered Ohio State University, majoring in Psychology as preparation for a career in personnel work. He was supported in school by the GI Bill, but he also had a series of temporary jobs including work as a "Photostat Operator" for Schiff Shoe, and a "Ward Attendant" for the Bureau of Juvenile Research in Columbus. He graduated in 1949 with a Bachelor of Arts degree. During the next two years, before gaining employment at Wright Patterson Air Force Base in Dayton, Ohio, he held a variety of temporary or short term positions, including an "Auto

Assembler" for Chrysler in Detroit; an "interviewer" for the Ohio State Employment Service in Toledo; a "game operator" at Coney Island; and for the Radio Amusement Company in New York he "made change."

Victor associated himself with a number of amateur theatres starting with the Springfield Ohio Civic Theatre and later in Washington, D.C., with the Unitarian Players and Theatre Lobby. Victor was a life-long stutterer, and while many people who stutter are able to speak memorized lines without revealing their malady, there is no evidence he performed on stage. He did, however, become a member of the Toastmasters. I learned of his interest in theatre in the 1950s when we both lived in Columbus and would travel to Yellow Springs to see plays at the Antioch Shakespeare Festival.

After six years in community theatre Victor's interests turned to genealogy, oil painting, photography, creative writing, mountaineering, and shooting. He became a knife collector and a gun collector and was a long time member of the National Rifle Association. He learned computer programming and as an avocation wrote programs for moving screen savers. For more than 35 years he was interested in astrology and created hundreds of astrological charts for family members, friends, politicians, entertainers and celebrities.

Besides the NRA, Victor was a Mason and a member of the Theosophical Society. In his last months he subscribed to Time Magazine, The New Yorker Magazine, and PC Digest. He did his own taxes, owned and drove a car. He lived alone in an apartment complex near the Pentagon, where he cooked for himself. He moved about the apartment with the aid of a walker and found that a wheelchair was the most convenient and comfortable way to sit.

I had visited Vic several times when I had business in Washington and we periodically talked on the telephone. He was a source of family history, having interviewed many of his father's generation in the late 1940s and early 1950s. Together, we were able to create stories for family members.

In Victor's octogenarian years, his health problems were frequent and severe. He suffered two heart attacks and two strokes; he had a prostate operation and a knee replacement. On December 5 of last year (2006) Victor telephoned me. His voice was raspy, shaky and his speech was hesitant, as if he found it difficult to say what was on his mind. He said that at age 86 he is "slowing down," and losing his sense of balance. He is considering going into a "home." I asked if he wanted me to come to Arlington and he said yes. I made arrangements to leave in two days, but Victor called on the next day and said that my astrological signs were not favorable for travel and I should delay the trip. It turned out that my travel day was a day of heavy snow with icy conditions in the mountains.

I did make the trip in January and brought back with me some of his drawings and paintings, photographs and negatives. We talked about finding a home in the Dayton area and listed the things that needed to be accomplished to make the move possible. The tentative date was set for the end of April after I returned from a five-week trip to Europe. Victor began paring down his possessions, but the task was overwhelming, even with the help of Hilda Bowden, his long serving housekeeper. When I came to Arlington in April I worked with Victor to shed possessions of lesser value, making many trips down the hall to the refuse chute. The last 24 hours before the movers came were extremely tense. Victor came to realize that he could not go through his papers and possessions one item at a time. It was time to let go of papers and possessions that had been a lifetime accumulation. This was very stressful, but the movers came on time, packing up those items that would go with us to Ohio.

The one-day drive on April 30 from Arlington, Virginia to One Lincoln Park (OLP) in Kettering, Ohio was very pleasant.

Victor was at ease, pleased to be traveling, and we chatted about many things: family history and stories, philosophy and religion, and matter-of-factly, death and dying. The one book he brought with him in the automobile was a book on Theosophy. He said that he did not fear dying and that when death came, he would go to sleep and his spirit would leave his body. It would be a peaceful transition. He also said that he was ready to leave this world, to which I took exception, saying the next three years of his life would be pleasant.

The spirit of relaxation that was manifest during the drive disappeared as we moved into the Lincoln Park apartment. I spent a great deal of time running errands to make the apartment comfortable and livable. I arranged with the Lincoln Park staff to make an appointment with a geriatric physician, but May 16 was the first available date. I compiled, from Victor's records, his medical and medication history. Victor irritated the OLP staff by making too many requests. I knew the move would be stressful, but not to the degree he exhibited. I expected that within a month or so, as he settled in and met other residents, he would be happy in his new abode. And indeed, he related to me that the other residents he had met in the dining room were very friendly, indeed, friendlier than the staff.

On the 16th of May, the OLP driver took Victor to Dr. Tamara Togliatti, but the medical records Victor and I had filled out together had not been delivered. The doctor found she was unable to make any diagnosis at that time as Victor was not articulate on this day and could not answer her questions. Another appointment was made for the following month.

Sometime on that day, May 16, Victor suffered a stroke, and whether it was before leaving OLP, or in the doctor's office, or afterwards, I don't know. That evening at 9:00 p.m., I received a call from the OLP desk requesting my assistance because Victor kept making requests they felt they could not honor. I came and took Victor for an automobile ride, which he found to be relaxing. I visited again on Thursday, but not on Friday as Sharon and I were preparing for a dinner party at our house.

At 3:45 p.m., on that Friday, the director of OLP telephoned saying that I must find a "temporary weekend" place for Victor because OLP did not have the staff to take care of him. She faxed a list of places that accept "Alzheimer patients." She admitted that Victor might not be readmitted to OLP. I told her it would be impossible for me to make any arrangement with such a short notice. We ended up hiring a special attendant at $20 per hour to stay with Victor until arrangements could be made. The next day, on Saturday, we took him to the Hospital Emergency room at Kettering Memorial Hospital. A CAT scan revealed a "cerebral hemorrhage." He was placed in intensive care where they attempted to stabilize his very high blood pressure. After three days in intensive care he was moved to a regular ward. The doctors determined that he needed a feeding tube, which if installed would permit Victor to be discharged to a nursing home.

On May 23 Victor was moved to Trinity Nursing Care in Beavercreek, a five-minute drive from my house. He was still able to respond to me and say my name, but he was sleeping more and more and was clearly losing vitality. "Hi, Vic", I would say, "Who am I?" and he would reply in a faint voice, "Abie." On Wednesday, Trinity had called to say that he had fallen out of his bed. On Friday, June 1, I received a call at 7:30 a.m. telling me that Victor's vital signs were failing. My daughter and I arrived at Trinity at 7:55. "Hello Vic, it's me, its Abe; can you hear me?" No response. At 8:00, my daughter noted that Vic was not breathing.

Victor passed away precisely as he said he would. Peacefully. The spirit left the body. I wondered if my greeting "Hello Vic, it's me, it's Abe" was permission to pass on to the next realm.

A number of people have commended me for becoming

involved in Victor's life, but it never occurred to me to do otherwise. Victor's brother Dewey, with whom I had a close relationship, had helped our dear Uncle Frank in his last years, eventually bringing Frank to Ohio, where he passed away. It was only fitting to be involved with Victor as Dewey was with Frank.

X | APPENDIX

FROM BARN TO THEATRE
A Department Chair's Career

By Eugene Cantelupe
Professor Emeritus
Wright State University

During 11 of the 18 years at Wright State University, my direct supervisor was Dr. Eugene Cantelupe, Dean of the College of Liberal Arts.

That present patrons of WSU Theatre, enjoying the personal and technological amenities of the Festival or Celebration Theatre, would believe that the University's first plays appeared in a grange hall on New Liberty Road, two miles west of the campus? From 1970 to 1974, in this barn like structure with wooden planks for seats and an improvised platform for a stage, plays by Aristophanes, Ibsen, O'Neill, and an occasional unknown playwright were produced and performed with imagination, enthusiasm, and much verve on the part of a few faculty members and student actors. Each performance was a sellout, immediately popular, then as now, with the campus and the community. From such meager beginnings did Dr. Abe Bassett in 1970 start his career at Wright State University as Director of Theatre in the Department of Speech and Theatre.

In 1974, the drama program moved into its present facility in the Creative Arts Center. Abe Bassett was appointed chair of the newly formed Department of Theatre Arts, assumed as well the responsibilities of producer and director. The standard and direction that he wished the program to take had already been set in the previous four years: plays were to be selected from the classical as well as the contemporary repertory, along with original and experimental works; each one to be designed, lighted, costumed, directed and acted at peak level of the talents that the faculty, staff, and students possessed.

This vision and drive for excellence Abe Bassett never compromised, never diminished. His seventeen years as chair have been threaded with one goal, one ambition: to forge the Department of Theatre Arts into not only the best department in the state but also one of the best departments in the United States. "One of the top ten drama departments in the country," Abe constantly, consistently repeated.

All who know and have worked with Abe Bassett during these years are aware of his personal and professional qualities: his imagination and wit; his energy and work habits that ignored both clock and schedule; his wide knowledge of academic theatre, its curriculum, and the need for a strict student regimen: his reaching always for the most and the best possible in program resources—faculty, staff, and equipment. His efforts never recognized obstacles or problems. And such there were for the University throughout the decade of the seventies: erratic enrollments; economic downturns in the state and the nation; shrinking state budgets and university allocations. However, the Department of Theatre Arts managed to develop in size, scope, and standard. With resources seldom, if ever, commensurate with the department's actual growth– the handful of faculty produced five or six plays a year—Dr. Bassett continued to recruit faculty with distinguished records of achievement in all aspects of Theatre—history, technology, and acting. He also attracted students far beyond the region and the state whose academic records and talents now equal and indeed exceed those of other students throughout the University; and he added to the department's curriculum the study of dance and film, thus making the program a rarity among drama departments in the nation and giving an added dimension to the schedule of productions, such as musicals, dance recitals, and film festivals.

The decade of the 80s has brought the recognitions and rewards that the chair and the department of Theatre Arts have long deserved. The Ohio Board of Regents, on three occasions, has singled out the department as one of Wright State University's programs of excellence, granting it sums for equipment, additional faculty, and visiting actors and directors for the stage, television and motions pictures. On the professional scene the department has received numerous awards from state and regional dramatic groups and organizations, the most illustrious among them from the American College Theatre Festival that invited the department, five times, to give performances in various localities. In April 1979, this nationally renowned organization invited the department to perform *Look Back in Anger* at the John F. Kennedy Center for the Performing Arts, Washington, D.C.

Thus, the goal and vision of excellence that Dr. Bassett held for the drama program from the very start of his career in 1970 has been realized, a lustrous attainment pursued not so much for himself as for the Department and the University, both of which have transcended scanty, meager beginnings. In this academic drama, Abe Bassett has played no small role.

WSU THEATER SHAPES UP ON PAPER

By Walt McCaslin
Journal Herald Columnist

Abe Bassett, the new director of the Wright State Players, admits to being eclectic in his theatrical outlook—and, if all goes well, he'll soon have a large and flexible building to be eclectic in.

He unrolled a sheaf of architect's drawings, construction of which could begin in the summer. He obviously was pleased by what had taken shape on paper, and felt that he and his department had played an important part in planning it.

It's a reward experience for a theater crew to be on hand when the building they will use is being debated and committed to blueprints. Both the architect and the administration have been willing to listen and make changes, said Bassett. They've been determined to "get it right"—and this should cheer any artist who, perhaps in the past, has run afoul of plant-and-equipment pedants.

Bassett is a man who seems unmolested by most of the psycho-socio nitpicking which can "blunt the native hue of resolution" and complicate enterprises of pith and moment. His simple undoubting theory is that Wright State will become the best, theatre department in Ohio. Though a former OSU man himself, he dismisses the theater there with a shrug.

.....

It's probably fair to conclude that Wright State will do some excellent work in the future, will develop rapidly as a training ground for the theatrical arts and crafts and will capture progressively larger audiences.

.....

We'll wait and see how it turns out.

A CAREER IN PUBLISHING

I began reading newspapers before I was ten years old. I was attracted to the sports page and their coverage of the Williamson Red Birds, champions of the Mountain State League. The star player was Stan Musial who was promoted to a higher league before the season ended. He was a St. Louis Cardinal, and that became my team. I rooted for Musial throughout his long professional career.

When World War broke out in December 1941, I read the Williamson *Daily News* for news about the war; the defeats and victories. I specifically remember the fear I had when in early 1942 (I was 11) the Pacific war was going poorly for the United States.

Papa sometimes asked me to read newspaper stories for him. This may have been because I could read faster than he could, or perhaps it was his way to encourage me to read.

On the two pages following, is Vol. I, No. 4 of a family newspaper I wrote, edited and "published" in April 1945 when I was 14. Inserting the page in landscape orientation and using the underline key produced those vertical lines. Because the typewriter ribbon had two colors, the top half black and the bottom half red, some headlines were printed in red.

The title of my newspaper should have been *The Bassettonian*, or even *Bassettainian*, but I didn't know better.

Later, when my high school sponsored a career day, I chose to hear what a professional reporter from the Columbus *Dispatch* had to say about the profession of newspaper reporting. He told us that most young people get their start working in the obituary department. That is when my interest in newspaper reporting faded.

IF YOU DONT WRITE YOUR WRONG

EXTRA

YOUR SEMI-MONTHLY
HOMES**NEWS

SUNDAY APRIL 22, 1945

RED STREAK EDITION

Vol. 1	BASSETTAIN	No1 4

BAND to GIVE ANNUAL CONCERT

The Williamson High school Band under the direction of Selma Bassett is to present its Eighth Annual Concert, Friday April 27. This years band composed of 34 playing members will play such pieces as "Barbar of Seville", "Hail W.Va.", "Saber and Spurs" And other pieces furnishing great Entertainment.

Eight pieces will also be played by the Junior Band (23 playing Members), the songs can be played with not too much difficulty for a group that hasnt practised for two months.

SYRIAN DELEGATE TO FRISCO CONFERENCE WELL KNOWN HERE
* * *

The Syrian delegation to the San Fransisco Conference will be headed by Berris Bak Kouri, a native of El Kafir and a uncle to Mrs. Eli Bassitt in Welch W.Va.

- - - -

LOCAL SOLDIER ON FURLOUGH AFTER LONG OVERSEAS SERVICE

Sgt. Mickey Smith, of the U.S. Army, is enjoying his first furlough since joining the service. He has been in Australia.

SENIOR PLAY IS A BIG SUCCESS

T

The Senior Class of 1945 put on the most successful play ever to be presented in Williamson High School. The play, "Little Women", by Louisa May Alcott, was under the direction of Miss Rose G. Smith. Friday night gate receipts totaled $375. and total expenditures totaled $230.

LOCAL STATION NOW ON MUTUAL HOOKUP
* * *

The local broadcasting station, WBTH, celebrated its sixth anniversary by joining the Mutual broadcasting system, Fri,. April 20. It is the only station in Southern W.Va. to be thus honored.

LOCAL PASTOR TO BE IN CHARGE OF CAMP
* * * * * *

The Rev. Fred. J.Virgin and his wife were asked to be in charge of the Girls' Episcopal Church Camp to be held at Cowen, W.Va. during the period of July 16 to July 28. Age limits are from 12 to 16. The camp, Camp Caesar, (Webster County 4-H Club) will be used by the Episcopal boys for a two-week period preceeding the girls.

STATE AND CITY HONORED

Master Sergeant Bentley K, Hurt, son of Mr. and Mrs. Roy B. Hurt, was one of eight servicemen who acted as pallbearers at the late Mr. Roosevelt's funeral. In a telephone call to his parents Sunday evening, Sgt. Hurt said it was an occasion he could never forget. He is stationed at Fort Myers. Virginia, His wife is the former Miss Gladys McCoy of this city. He served in the honor guard, in Wash., DC for King George VI and Queen Elizabeth of England when they visited here before the present war. Shortly after entering the Army he was a member of the Honor Guard for the late Queen Marie of Rummania, and her daughter Princess Eleana.

His brother, Charles Hurt, USN, lost his life when his ship was torpedoed en route to Iceland. He has a sister Mrs. Kenneth Bandy, who is the former Miss Eleanor Hurt.

* * * *

STAFF

Editor--Abe Bassett
Ass't. Editor and Typist--Lorraine B.
Guest Editor--Virginia Caudill Smith
Reporter--Abe Bassett

- - - - - - - -

BASSETTIAN   SUNDAY APRIL 22   Page two

LOCAL POOL WILL NOT OPEN

****

Due to the shortage in the water supply, the municipal swimming pool will not be open this summer, Mayor J. Matt Smith announced. This will be a tough break for the kiddies as well as the adult swimmers, as the pool was one of the chief means of recreation. But the Williamson folk can't be licked. They will take Lick Creek on the KY. side and Cabwaylingo on the W.Va. side.

------------------*

One of the main places of recreation this summer will be the skating rink at West Williamson.

*------------ *

The Board of Education has repaired the pool at the High School so as to prevent the youngsters from going to Lick Creek too much, as it has proved a dangerous place. One boy was killed last year there.

****

DIOCESE ACQUIRES NEW CAMP

The Episcopal Diocese of W.Va. has bought a new camp site in the eastern panhandle of W.Va. at the price of $10,000. The camp is far over 500 acres, has several lakes and a beautiful landscape. The camp will probably be in operation next summer.

****

OUR GOLD STAR ***

NEW TRADE SCHOOL WILL OPEN IN JULY

*********   ********

The new Trade School, which has been under construction since last summer will open in JULY. The Board of Education will occupy a room on the upper floor as its new office.

- - - - - - - -

WHS TO FIELD BASE* - BALL TEAM --

Williamson High School will field a baseball team composed of the high school athletes, under the coaching of Mervin Varney and Ben Hamilton. Although a very good team is expected it will probably not enter the state elimination tournament in Charleston, W.Va. because of the extreme difficulty in building a won-lost record in such a brief time. Coach Varney has been attempting to engage in games with such major teams as East and Central High Schools in Huntington.

PERSONALS

***

Miss Selma Bassett has accepted a job as waterfront director at a Girl Scout Camp near Pikeville, Ky.

- - - - - -

Miss Gladys Bassett has accepted and begun organizing the GFS in the Episcopal Church. The club has been without a sponsor for several years.

- - - - - -

Miss Lorraine Bassett was elected Secretary of the GFS at a recent meeting. Other officers are as follows: Pres.-Gloria Mickel V.Pres.-Marg. Buck Sed'y- L. Bassett Treas.- Jeanette Cantees Publicity Agent-- Adele Ammar.

- - - - - -

Two radios and a phonograph were sold last week. (The money was very welcome.)

- - - - - -

Miss Gladys Bassett was honored this evening by a birthday dinner. Mrs. Virginia Caudill Smith was present as a guest. The honoree was showered with several lovely gifts .

- - - - - -

BIG   JOKE !!
1-2-3-4-5-6-7,
All good Bassetts' go to Heaven, When they get there, they will say, Canteeses' went the other way. (Official Bassett slogan) Ha Ha Ha

****

BIKING ACROSS AMERICA
An interview with Abe Bassett by Abe Bassett

Q. I understand you have been on a long bicycle trip?
Yes, I just completed a coast-to-coast bicycle trip that started in Carlsbad, California, just north of San Diego and ended in St. Simon's Island, just east of Brunswick, Georgia.

Q. How long was the trip?
We covered nearly 2500 miles in 35 riding days with four days of rest. We started on Sunday, March 23, 1997, resting the next four Sundays, and ended on Wednesday, April 30. We biked the first eight and the last 10 days consecutively.

Q. How far did you travel each day?
We averaged more than 71 miles a day, but our two longest days were 94 and 95 miles. During the last 10 days, we had days of 94, 92, 82, and 81 miles, but by that time we had become strong riders and had reached relatively flat terrain, so that was no big deal.

Q. Was the biking hard? Weren't there a lot of mountains to bike through?
Yes, the biking was hard and the mountains were substantial. We climbed more than 60,000 feet during the trip.

Q. Where were the toughest mountains?
The most anticipated mountain was Cloudcroft just east of Alamogordo, New Mexico. Here we had a 16-mile grade in which we climb 4315 vertical feet, without a single level spot. The Cloudcroft mountain pass is 8650 feet above sea level. Fortunately for us, it was a beautiful day, with a temperature in the low 50s at the top—an ideal day for biking.

We were advised to put the bikes in the lowest gear and to take our time. This was good advice: it took about three hours to complete the climb, and it was tiring but not exhausting.

There were several other tough climbs: to Julian, California; from Superior to Globe, Arizona; and surprisingly, in east Alabama.

Q. Alabama?

Right. There was a series of hills with steep grades. We call these "grinders" because before you reached the one-third mark, you had to move to your lowest gear and "grind" your way to the top. These hills went on for about 50 miles, but it felt like a thousand.

Q. How did your body react to the stress of all this biking?

We generally ate dinner at 6:00 p.m. and were in bed between 8:00 and 9:00 p.m. I fell asleep quickly every night. After several weeks, I learned how to massage my legs at night and again during the morning to alleviate the stiffness (and a buildup of lactic acid). I was always a little stiff in the morning, but after 30 to 40 minutes of biking, I had recovered. During the trip I lowered my body fat by 8%, and lost 14 pounds. The first four days at home, I not only slept long nights, but also was sleepy throughout the day.

Q. How is it sitting on those little bicycle seats?

In Apache Junction, Arizona, we ran across an itinerant biker—a homeless biker by choice—who had been on the road for three years. When I asked if his "butt" hurt, he said "no." But when I asked how long he biked before it stopped hurting, he said "two and one-half years."

Oh, yeah, my butt really hurt for the first two weeks. Actually, it is not the "butt" that hurts. It was a spot high up on my inner thighs where chafing took place. Once they become sensitive, you have a problem until the skin toughens up.

I used Bag Balm during the day to provide lubrication for the skin and Desenex at night to promote healing. Halfway through the trip, I purchased a shock-absorbing seat post to reduce road vibration and jolting. My last three weeks on the bike were relatively pleasant.

Q. *What kind of bicycle did you ride? Was it a mountain bike?*
No, I rode a 58cm "road bike" with 27" wheels and 24 gears, made by Trek. The frame is made of carbon fiber for its lightweight and resiliency, and it has a "granny" gear, which was mandatory for the steeper grades.

Q. *How many people were with you?*
We had 37 bikers who went coast to coast, and about five other people who, by design, went part of the way.

Q. *Who organized the trip?*
Wandering Wheels in Upland, Indiana. Their leader, Bob Davenport, has made more than 50 coast- to-coast trips. They offer tours the year around. This was my fourth trip with Wandering Wheels but my first coast-to-coast.

Q. *What services do they offer?*
There was a "sag wagon," a van that carried water, tools, spare tubes and tires, which would transport bicycles and people if they were injured or sick. Wheels also furnished 13 meals a week, usually breakfasts and suppers. And they had an excellent mechanic to repair and adjust our bikes. Finally, several staff rode with us, and they were ready to assist with flat tires, or to give advice. There were seven staff and 37 riders. Four of the staff rode the entire distance.

Q. *You didn't ride the interstate highways, did you?*
Actually, because there were no alternative routes, we did ride two interstate stretches, one in Arizona and one in New Mexico.

Q. *Was that pleasant?*
Well, the pavement is relatively smooth, the shoulders are
wide, and the grades are tempered, but you have to contend
with rumble strips, road debris, traffic noise, and sometimes
the wind shock that comes from a 20-wheel tractor-trailer
traveling at high speed.

Q. *Which of those is worst?*
Each in turn is worst. The Arizona rumble strips were deep
diagonal grooves that could not be escaped, so every eight
seconds your biked rocked and rolled over a three-inch wide
groove, one inch deep. That day, road debris contributed to
a total of 29 flat tires. The culprit is the shred of steel from
truck's steel-belted radial tires that explode, and are left on the
highway. One shard of steel that caused a flat on my bike was
only of an inch long, and very small in diameter.

Until you have biked across America, you have no idea how
much glass is on highway shoulders, and you would be amazed
at the number of bolts I spotted. These bolts ranged from ¾ of
an inch that may have fallen from auto oil pans, to some 12-
inch bolts. I suspected many came from muffler hangers. I saw
hundreds of bolts, but only one nut.

We came across about eight places on highway shoulders
where vehicles had burned. You could tell by the deeply
scarred and discolored asphalt.

One of my fellow riders counted "road kill" that included "a
road runner in New Mexico, two coyotes in Texas, a squashed
alligator and a flattened bear in Louisiana, a dead copperhead
and deer in Alabama, a water moccasin that bared its fangs
and a dead beaver in Georgia."

Q. *Did you have time to see sights along the way?*
Oh, sure, we toured White Sands National Monument, the
Okefenokee Swamp Park in Georgia, and the Kennedy
Museum in the Texas Book Depository in Dallas. We stopped

in the small towns to enjoy the unusual attractions like the Chamber of Commerce building in Grand Saline, Texas, which is built of blocks of salt. In Mineola, Texas, we stopped at a most unique retail establishment: Kitchen's Hardware and Delicatessen, where I sampled their homemade blackberry cobbler and had a bottle of Sarsaparilla soda. In Marshall, Texas, we attended a gospel music festival.

Q. *How were you treated by the drivers of trucks and cars?*

Generally, we were well treated. We were warned that some of the commercial truckers would be resentful that we were taking their space on the highway, but dozens of times, we received friendly toots from the truckers. The same was true of car drivers.

On April 1 and 2, when we were in Arizona, we had to contend with the hundreds of "snow birds" who were moving their RVs and trailers eastward. Some of these folks did not seem aware of the width of their vehicles. But most drivers steered wide of us, often moving their cars and trucks to the left of the centerline, when traffic permitted.

We had more trouble east of the Mississippi, where some drivers seemed to ignore our presence on the highway, and where shoulder width was narrower or didn't exist. We always rode on the shoulder, or when there was no shoulder, we hugged the white line. In Louisiana, Mississippi, and Alabama, I learned to get off my bike whenever logging trucks, or trucks pulling one of those 14-foot wide prefabricated homes, was going to pass.

Q. *Didn't you ride any roads "less-traveled by?"*

Oh, sure, and we loved it. To be able to hear the birds sing and dogs bark. Given a choice, we would all prefer the quieter road.

Q. *How do you watch for traffic coming up behind you?*
We had mirrors attached to the bicycle, our glasses, or to our
helmet. I was always aware of approaching vehicles. When
two or more riders were together, the person in the rear would
shout "car back," and we would immediately move to the
right. I learned early on that when I saw only one vehicle in
my mirror, not to assume there was only one vehicle. Many
times, a second car would be tailgating the first, or a smaller
car would be hidden behind a van or truck. The drivers of the
second vehicle were often not aware they were approaching
bicyclists.

Q. *Were there a lot of dogs? Did they chase you?*
I think that in Texas, in order to be a citizen, it is mandatory
that you own a pickup truck with a large dog riding in the back.
And in Alabama, you must own three to five dogs and have a
hole in your fence, so the dogs can chase passing cyclists. Or so
it seemed.

We were chased several times, but most dogs don't run
beyond their master's property. So most of us kick up our speed
and race away. Well before the end of the trip, a barking dog
had no effect on my adrenalin.

Q. *Did anybody get hurt on your trip?*
Several people had falls, so there were some scraped knees and
shins. One female rider hit a dog and received a nasty gash just
below her elbow, and our leader crashed when, at 23 mph, he
lost control of his bike and ran off the road into a ditch. I said
to him that he crashed with style and grace, and he laughed.
I fell once when I came to a stop and had difficulty getting
my shoe out of the pedal clip. Happily, everyone who started
completed the tour.

Q. *What was the hardest day?*
There were two particularly hard days. The first was the 78

miles into Lordsburg, New Mexico, when we faced a headwind that blew from 25 to 35 miles per hour. It was very discouraging to work so hard to achieve a speed of only 5 miles an hour.

In New Mexico, when we left Artesia for Hobbs, it was 36 degrees, the humidity was 100 percent, there was a headwind, the pavement was rough, and there was a slight upgrade. That's five negative factors. I would have rather stayed in bed that day.

Q. Did you ride every day?

No, from Lamesa to Roby, in West Texas, we were transported by van. A "blue northern" swooped down upon us with strong headwinds producing a wind-chill factor of minus three degrees. Biking in those conditions would have been foolhardy.

We got caught in a terrific thunderstorm in Louisiana. My riding partner that day, a veterinarian from Orange County, California, was fearful of the prospect of tornadoes, so he rode as fast as he could through the rain storm, ignoring the torrent of lighting all around him. Later, I explained to him that one can see and hear a tornado, but one does not see lighting strike you. We found out that there were 4000 lightning strikes in that storm.

Q. Where did you stay at night?

We stayed in motels seven nights, one university and one primary school, we camped seven nights, but mostly we stayed in churches, mainly Baptist and Methodist. Sometimes I would choose to spend the night in a tent rather than be indoors.

I recall fondly the night in Mineola, Texas, where we stayed in a small country church. It was a beautiful clear evening with a full moon and the Hale-Bopp comet in the sky. On the other side of the church in his tent was "Fritz," who began playing his harmonica. He was soon joined in his plaintive music by the howling of coyotes. This was a scene for the movies.

Q. *What did Wandering Wheels feed you?*
Hydrocarbons were featured. For breakfast, we had oatmeal
and cream of wheat every morning, supplemented with baked
goods, pancakes, waffles, milk, juice, coffee, bananas, oranges
and apples. Evening meals included pork chops, beef, tuna
fish and pasta. Every supper had a dessert. We had great
quantities of food and we needed it because we were burning
as many as 8000 calories a day.

**Q. *What kind of reactions did you receive from people
you met?***
Amazement, wonder, admiration, and sometimes puzzlement
were the common reactions. But one incredulous lady asked,
"What did you people do before you lost your minds?" Along
the way, people asked a lot of questions; it surprised them that
anybody would want to bike across America. I often invited
them to join us when we started out the next morning, but to a
person, they said they couldn't go more than a couple of blocks.

Our entire troupe took delight in answering the questions
posed to us by people, young and old alike.

Q. *Why did you do this trip?*
I was motivated by the physical and psychological challenge.
When I started out, I honestly didn't know if I could make it.
Could I really bike 725 miles in ten consecutive days? Could
I climb up 7% grades that went on for miles? Would my seat
and hands and knees survive the ordeal? Was I going to be
warm and dry? Could I cope with the days of tough head winds?
Would I like the strangers with whom I would travel with for
the next six weeks?

I was interested in the challenge, and now I am very pleased
to have met that challenge.

Q. *Are you now glad you went on the trip?*
During the last three weeks of the trip I kept thinking that I
was glad I came but having done it, I didn't need to do it again.

Within one week of returning home, however, I began thinking I might like to do the northern coast-to-coast, from Seattle to the Atlantic, or the border-to-border, from Florida to Canada. I guess a challenge met needs to be followed by more difficult challenge.

I have learned a lot about preparation, and about bicycle techniques, and I would be better prepared for the next trip.

Q. *What are your goals for the immediate future?*
I am determined that I will maintain my weight loss. I am down to the weight I carried through most of my working adult life, and about 30 pounds less than what I weighed 11 months ago.

Q. *How did you prepare yourself for the coast-to-coast trip? Had you done a lot of riding beforehand?*
I rode very little beyond the 400-mile Wandering Wheel January trip, from Cocoa Beach to Key West. Starting on November 1, 1996 I was in the gym four to five times a week, working on aerobics and weights. My physical improvement was noticeable and as it turned out I started the trip in reasonably good shape, considering my age and weight. However, I led a 17-day tour to London and Paris immediately before the bike trip, and I was afraid I would lose the edge of what I had attained.

Q. *Did you?*
I didn't gain weight because I walked a lot, and I climbed stairs at every opportunity. Our room was on the 10th floor and some days, I walked up and down six times.

Q. *Do I understand that you flew from Paris directly to California?*
Almost. I stopped over in Beavercreek for about 12 hours; just enough time to pay some bills and repack my clothes. I had already shipped my bicycle, tent, sleeping bag, and biking clothes.

Q. Tell me about yourself.

I have lived in Beavercreek since 1971 with my wife Sharon, who is the Deputy Executive Director of St. Joseph Children's Treatment Center in Dayton. Our two children, Douglas and Valerie, are graduates of Beavercreek High School.

For eighteen years I was a Professor of Theatre at Wright State University and for most of those years, I was Chairman of the Department of Theatre Arts. I retired from WSU in 1988 to accept the position of Dean, School of Fine and Performing Arts at Indiana University- Purdue University Fort Wayne. I retired from there in 1994 returning to Beavercreek. During my Indiana years, I maintained my home in Beavercreek. Since retirement, I have formed a travel company, Bassett Tours, and each year I develop and lead tours to London and to the Middle East.

Q. How much biking have you done in the three months since the end of the coast-to-coast?

By the middle of August I had biked about 900 miles. My average trip was about 45 to 50 miles. I biked to Milford and back on the Little Miami Bike Trail, a distance of 81 miles. And I did a three-day trip loop to Bellefontaine, Columbus and Beavercreek, a distance of 210 miles. I expect to bike once or twice a week until sometime in November or December, depending on weather conditions.

Q. What did you learn about bicycling since the coast-to-coast trip?

I have learned a lot. I have had more time to assimilate the lessons learned on the trip, and to make further adjustments.

When I started the coast-to-coast trip I had to adjust to a new bicycle, a new shifting system, a new helmet, new toeless clips, a new tent, a new rear view mirror. When I think back on it, I am amazed I did as well as I did. I would say I have moved from being an "advanced beginner" to a "good intermediate" rider.

CURRICULUM VITAE: FINAL EDITION

What follows on the next five pages is my last curriculum vitae. It is the record of the academic years that constitutes my adult working life. This CV was prepared when I was Dean of the College of Visual and Performing Arts at Indiana University-Purdue University in Fort Wayne (IPFW).

I had retired from Wright State University in Dayton in 1988 to accept the position in Indiana, retiring from that institution in 1994. After selling my condominium in Fort Wayne, I returned home to Beavercreek. Sharon had remained there, continuing to work at St. Joseph's Children Treatment Center, which she did for another three years, retiring in 1997.

In academia, one always upgrades their resume or curriculum vita. In my files is a copy of my first resume, when there were very few things to distinguish one's record. In those early days, it was necessary to include information that is now, for good reason, illegal.

That includes:
- A photograph (to prove we were white and looked normal);
- Your family status (to make the point we were family men who needed the income to support our family and were less likely to have dalliances with undergraduate students); and
- Your religious preferences (even if we didn't have one), to prove we were not Jewish or atheists, depending on the nature of the institution. (At the time, Muslims were not part of the consciousness of society.)

Such were the prejudices of the times, particularly when one applied for a position in a smaller, more provincial institution.

ABE J. BASSETT

Résumé

Personal Data

Dean, and Professor of Theatre
School of Fine and Performing Arts
Indiana University-Purdue University
Fort Wayne, IN 46805-1499
(219) 481-6977

5717 Port Royal
Fort Wayne, IN 46815
(219) 486-1333
Married (1959)
Two Adult Children

Education

Doctor of Philosophy, The Ohio State University, Columbus, Ohio
Master of Arts, The Ohio State University, Columbus, Ohio
Certificate, University of Paris (Sorbonne), Paris, France
Bachelor of Arts, Bowling Green State University, Bowling Green, Ohio
Diploma, Upper Arlington High School, Columbus, Ohio

Employment Chronology

1988-	Dean, School of Fine and Performing Arts, Indiana University-Purdue University, Fort Wayne, Indiana
1970-1988	Wright State University, Dayton, Ohio
74-88	Chairman, Department of Theatre Arts
72-74	Chairman, Department of Speech and Theatre
70-72	Director of Theatre, Professor of Theatre
1968-1970	Dickinson State College, Dickinson, North Dakota Professor and Chairman, Department of Theatre
1964-1968	Pacific Lutheran University, Tacoma, Washington Assistant Professor of Speech and Theatre
1963-1964	Westminster College and William Woods College, Fulton, Missouri Inter-college Coordinator and Director of Theatre
1960-1963	Central Missouri State University, Warrensburg, Missouri, Director of Radio, Assistant Professor of Speech and Theatre
1958-1960	Producer, Writer, Announcer, WOSU-AM-FM-TV, Columbus, Ohio
1952-1954	United States Army, Special Services, Armed Forces Radio Network

Awards and Honoraries

1982	Outstanding Achievement Award, Ohio Theatre Alliance
1981	AMOCO Award of Excellence, American College Theatre Festival
1967	Alpha Phi Omega (National Theatre Honorary)
1951	Psi Chi (National Psychology Honorary)
1951	Alpha Psi Omega (National Service Honorary)

Abe J. Bassett   2

1950   Theta Alpha Phi (National Theatre Honorary)
1950   Sigma Rho Mu (Radio-Television Honorary)

Publications

"Memories of Rahija," Editor, Fort Wayne, In., 1992
"Kfeirian Reunion Foundation Newsletter," Editor and Publisher, 5 issues, 1989-1991
"Speaking of the Dean," ArtScene, Quarterly Newsletter of the School of Fine and
    Performing Arts, 8 issues, 1989-1992
"Producer's Notes," OnStage Program Guide, 25 issues, 1983-1987
"Equus: A Case for Censorship?," Association for Communication Administration
    Bulletin, Annadale, Virginia, March, 1986
"Collegiate Theatre: Alive, Diverse, and Thriving," ArtSpace, Ohio Arts Council, Vol. 8,
    No. 5, November/December, 1985
"Academic Challenge" Grant Application, October, 1985
"George Grizzard: A Professional on Campus," Dramatics Magazine, March, 1985
"The Ohio Theatre Alliance Playbill and Directory of Colleges and Universities," Editor,
    1987, 1986, 1985, 1984, 1983, 1982, 1981, 1980
"Program Excellence" Grant Application, co-authored with Charles Derry, January, 1984
"Viewpoints: Preparing for College," Secondary School Theatre Journal, Spring, 1981
"Theatre Programs in Ohio High Schools," The Ohio Theatre Alliance, 1975,
    (unpublished)
Book Review: Your Role in Oral Interpretation by Virgil D. Sessions and Jack B.
    Holland, in The Speech Teacher, Winter, 1968
Book Review: William Charles Macready: The Eminent Tragedian by Alan S.
    Downer, in the Educational Theatre Journal, March, 1967
"Macready's Coriolanus: An Early Contribution to the Modern
    Theatre," The OSU Theatre Collection Bulletin, 1964
The Actor-Manager Career of William Charles Macready, dissertation, The Ohio State
    University, 1962
"The Capitol Setting in Julius Caesar," The OSU Theatre Collection Bulletin, 1959
The Staging of Bulwer-Lytton's Richelieu, Lady of Lyons, and Money, thesis, The Ohio
State University, 1957

Panels, Adjudications, Conferences, Addresses, Consultancies

"Time Management for Academic Administrators," Indiana University-Purdue University,
    Fort Wayne, 1990, 1991
"How Faculty Regard Public Relations," Indiana University Public Relations Conference,
    May 31, 1990, Indianapolis
"The Value of Arts-In-Education," Fort Wayne Leadership Seminar, April 14, 1990

"Effective Utilization of Time," seminar for the Art Museum of Fort Wayne, October,
    1989

"Time Management for Academics and Professionals," Workshop, Southeastern Theatre Conference, Louisville, KY, March, 1989

Consultant, Upper Management Attitudes, Alabama Shakespeare Festival, December, 1988

"Ethics in Recruitment," Chair and Panelist, Southeastern Theatre Conference, Atlanta, Georgia, March, 1988

"Excellence in Theatre Training Programs," Panelist, Southeastern Theatre Conference, Atlanta, Georgia, March, 1988

"Fund for the Improvement of Post-Secondary Education (FIPSE) Advisory Committee on Program Assessment," Ohio Board of Regents, 1988-1990

"Law and the Arts," Dayton Lawyers Club, February, 1988

"Unique Marketing Approaches," Ohio Association of College Registrars and Admission Directors, Oxford, Ohio, November, 1987

"Contribution of Educational Theatre to the Community," Dayton Leadership Conference, Dayton, October, 1987

Consultant, Ohio Board of Regents, Program Excellence, May, 1987

Consultant, Ball State University, Program Review, April, 1987

Consultant, International Thespian Society, Cincinnati, January, 1987

Consultant, Time Management, Computer Usage, Alabama Shakespeare Festival, December, 1986

"What Do You Do When They Say No," Ohio Theatre Alliance Conference, Cincinnati, Ohio, October, 1986

"The College Theatre Program," Ohio Thespian Society Conference, Fairborn, Ohio, April, 1986

"Assertive Personal Marketing," Southeastern Theatre Conference, Charlotte, North Carolina, March, 1986

"Cultural Amenities in Dayton," Panelist, Leadership Dayton Program, September, 1985

"The Use of Computers in Theatre Administration," Panelist, Speech Communication Association, Chicago, November, 1984

"Equus and The Maturing of a University," Beavercreek Rotary Club, October, 1984

"Electronic Spreadsheets for Educators and Theatre Administrators,"Ohio Theatre Alliance, Columbus, Ohio, October, 1984

"The Arts in Education," The Civitan Club of Dayton, September, 1984

"Advising the Professionally Oriented Student," American Theatre Association, San Francisco, August, 1984

"The Hot L Baltimore," Promotion and Tenure Evaluation, Bowling Green State University, October, 1983

Adjudicator, International Thespian Society Conference, Muncie, Indiana, 1982

"How Should We Be Training People for the Theatre," Chair, Ohio Theatre Alliance, October, 1982, Westerville, Ohio

Adjudicator, Association of Community Theatres of Cincinnati, May, 1982

"Marketing the Arts," Ohio Regional Association of Concert and Lecture Enterprises (O.R.A.C.L.E.), Dayton, Ohio, October, 1981

Conference Coordinator and Program Chairman, Great Lakes Regional Theatre

Conference, American Theatre Association, and Ohio Theatre Alliance/United States
Institute for Theatre Technology, Fall Conference, October, 1981
Adjudicator, FACT Festival, Ohio Community Theatre Association, Columbus, 1979
"Does Anyone Know You're There?," Ohio Theatre Alliance, Panelist, Toledo, Ohio,
    April, 1979
Festival Coordinator and Program Chairman, American College Theatre Festival,
    Dayton, Ohio, 1977, 1988
"Theatre and Drama in the Schools: Report of State Survey," Ohio Theatre Alliance,
    Westerville, Ohio, 1975
"A Strategy for Improving Theatre in the Secondary Schools," Ohio Theatre Alliance,
    1975
"College and University Theatre Programs," Ohio Thespian Society, 1975
Adjudicator, University/Regional Theatre Association, Columbus, Ohio, 1976
Adjudicator, Ohio Theatre Alliance High School Play Festival, 1980, 1977, 1974

Offices in National and State Organizations

1981-1983 Governor, University College Theatre Association, American Theatre
           Association, Region III
1980-1982 Ohio Citizens Committee for the Arts, Executive Vice President
1979-1981 Ohio Alliance for Arts in Education, Vice President
1978-1979 Past President, Ohio Theatre Alliance
1977-1978 President, Ohio Theatre Alliance
1976-1978 American College Theatre Festival, Great Lakes Region, Executive
           Committee
1975-1976 Chairman, Heads Action Group, Ohio Theatre Alliance
1974-1975 Treasurer, Ohio Theatre Alliance
1973-1974 Treasurer, Ohio Theatre Alliance
1971-1972 Founding Constitutional Committee, Ohio Theatre Alliance

Service in Arts Organizations

1989   Fort Wayne Youth Theatre, Board of Directors
1988-   Community Arts Council
1988-1990 Forte Arts Festival, Steering Committee
1988-1990 Arts United, Planning Committee
1988-1990 Fort Wayne Ballet, Board of Directors, Marketing, Personnel Committees
1985-1986 Ohio Theatre Alliance, Development Committee
1981-1987 Dayton Ballet Company, Board of Trustees,
           Committees: Finance, Touring, Strategic Planning, School Victory Theatre
           Association, Program Committee
1977-1978 State Superintendent of Public Instruction's Forum on Arts in Education
1975-1976 Dayton Contemporary Dance Company, Board of Trustees
1975-1976 Advisory Board, Career Education in the Performing Arts, Centerville School

District, Centerville, Ohio
1973-1977 Dayton Youth Theatre, Board of Trustees

Selected Accomplishments as Founding Chairman
in the Department of Theatre Arts
at Wright State University

1988   Program Excellence Award
1985-1987 Planner for Creative Arts Center, II
1985-1991 Academic Challenge Award
1984-1985 Program Excellence Award
1973-1987 Chairman of Department from inception
1976-1987 Organizer of Annual High School Theatre Arts Workshop
1970-1987 Producer of 188 productions
1973-1980 Producing Director, SummerFun Summer Theatre
1974-1987 Producer, Touring Children's Theatre
1980-1987 Developer of Theatre Arts Endowment Funds
1970-1972 Planner for Creative Arts Center

Representative Courses Taught

Acting, Advanced Acting, Acting Seminar. Television Acting, Voice in Performance, Stage Dialects, Phonetics, Oral Interpretation, Oral Reading of Drama, Directing, Introduction to Theatre, Theatre History, Theatrical Criticism, Play Production, History of Broadcasting, Writing for Broadcasting, Educational Broadcasting, Mass Media, Radio and Television Production, Fundamentals of Speech, Public Address

Plays Directed

Antigone, Ah, Wilderness!, And They Dance Real Slow in Jackson, And Miss Reardon Drinks a Little, The Amorous Flea, Arsenic and Old Lace, The Bald Soprano, Blithe Spirit, Brigadoon, Brighton Beach Memoirs, Bus Stop, Carousel, Come Blow Your Horn, A Different Drummer, A Doll's House, Equus, Extremities, Five Fingers Exercise, The Good Doctor, Guys and Dolls, Hello Out There, In White America, Life With Father, Little Mary Sunshine, Mary, Mary, The Most Happy Fella!, The Miracle Worker, The Rainmaker, Riders to the Sea, The Runner Stumbles, South Pacific, Song of Norway, Scapino!, The Subject Was Roses, Summertree, A Shot in the Dark, A Thurber Carnival, The Taming of the Shrew, Twelfth Night, Romeo and Juliet, Spoon River Anthology, A View From the Bridge, Whose Life Is It Anyway?, The World of Carl Sandburg, 110 in the Shade

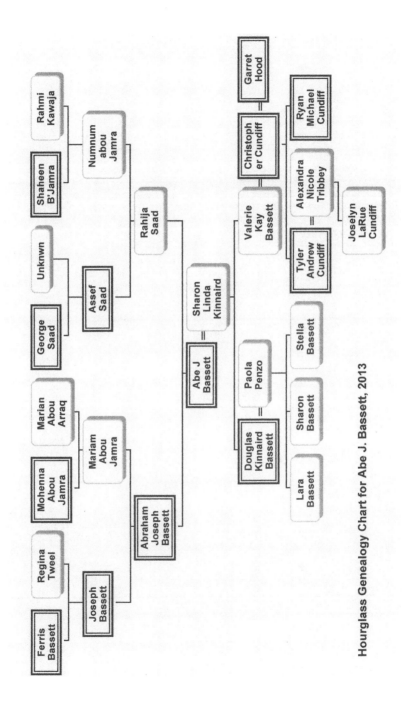

Hourglass Genealogy Chart for Abe J. Bassett, 2013

AN EPILOGUE: OBITUARY

ABE J. BASSETT

Abe J. Bassett (nee Abraham Joseph Bassett, Jr.), age 99, died suddenly and peacefully September 26, 2029 at home in Beavercreek, Ohio. Abe was born September 27, 1930 in Williamson, West Virginia, to Abraham and Rahija Saad Bassett, both immigrants from Kfeir, Lebanon. Interested in genealogy he established his family's descent from the ancient Phoenicians. Abe graduated from Upper Arlington High (OH) School in 1948, and Bowling Green State University in 1952. As a Corporal in the U.S. Army he served in Okinawa with the Armed Forces Radio Service, and acted the role of Capt. Fisby in the long running army production of *Teahouse of the August Moon*. Following service, he moved to San Francisco, and later to Europe where he studied at the University of Paris. Entering Ohio State University, he earned a Master's degree in 1957 and a Ph.D. in 1962 in Theatre History. He began a 34 year teaching career in 1960 at Central Missouri State University. He also taught at Pacific Lutheran University, Dickinson (ND) State University, and in 1970, came to Wright State University where he became the founding chair of the award winning Department of Theatre Arts. In 1988 he became founding Dean of the School of Fine and Performing Arts at Indiana-Purdue University, Fort Wayne, retiring in 1994. He was recognized as Emeritus Professor of Theatre from Wright State University.

Abe was known as a hard working teacher and administrator, a caring mentor, and a sensitive director of plays. He described himself as an artist and teacher, and one who was equally right and left brained. His friendships with students continued throughout his lifetime. He adored his lovely wife of 75 years, Sharon Kinnaird, whom he married in 1959, and their two children, Douglas (Paola) and Valerie Hood (Garret), and five grandchildren, Tyler and Ryan Cundiff, and Lara, Sharon and Stella Bassett of Milano, Italy. An avid traveler, he visited all 50 states, and 41 countries on five continents. For 21 years, he led Theatre and Art tours to London and Europe and to the Middle East. As an outdoorsman, he undertook three coast-to-coast bicycle trips, and once scaled Mt. Whitney in California.

Of all his loves was the love of his wife, parents, five sisters, three nieces and six nephews, and 17 grand nieces and nephews and many great grand nieces and nephews. He lived his life happily and fully, always looking forward to visits with friends and family.

399 words. Place in Dayton Daily News. Fort Wayne Journal Gazette; Williamson Daily News, Use photo. Drafted July 7, 2006